Last Writings

of

Richard L. "Arf" Epstein

The moral rights of the author have been asserted.

Names, characters, and incidents relating to any of the characters in this text are used fictitiously, and any resemblance to actual persons, living or dead, is entirely coincidental. *Honi soit qui mal y pense*.

Advanced Reasoning Forum
P. O. Box 635
Socorro, NM 87801   USA
www.AdvancedReasoningForum.org

paperback ISBN 978-1-938421-73-0

e-book ISBN 978-1-938421-74-7

Last Writings

Addiction studies
Teaching Addicts 2
Evaluating Treatments for Addiction 11
Addiction in the Body—Too Good Is Just Awful 27

Poems and . . .
Dog Day's Song 48
The ferret, the spider, ... 49
These days the spirit tries to rest 50
I have called 51
California is not London 52
Hope—a diptych 53
Monday Night at the Observatory 54
If we were all birds 55
Five poems in the style of the Chinese 56

Stories and . . .
Jewish Dogs 59
Youth 61
Arfito to Uschi 66
The Devil's Dictionary—an update 68
Shakespeare and dogs 71

Plays
The Hanging Tree 75
Princess 99
Ralph 105
My Fight with the Alligators 109
Spiridon 147

Essays in logic and philosophy
Three Questions about Logic 194
Is There a Problem with Formal Semantics for Natural Languages? 199
Mechanical ≠ Computable 206

Intentions	210
Numbers?	223
The Twenty-First or "Lost" Sophism on Self-Reference of John Buridan	242
The Procrastination Paradox	246

Preface

These writings were compiled by Richard L. "Arf" Epstein as ones he felt were sufficiently developed to be shared. Here are his comments.

Addiction studies

Teaching Addicts
    Written in July, 2017. Couldn't figure out where to publish it.

Evaluating Treatments for Addiction
    Written in May, 2018, and revised thereafter.

Addiction in the Body
    The first draft of this was written in 2017. After going over it with a brain-science class at New Mexico Tech, reading it out loud with a 9th-grade health sciences class at Socorro High School, getting comments from friends and colleagues, and recording it with Frencie Deters, it's been revised to what's here now. All attempts at getting funding for drawing the cartoons failed.

Poems

Dog Day's Song
    Written in Berkeley, California 1972.

The ferret, the spider, the dog . . .
    Written in Berkeley, California about 1984.

These days the spirit tries to rest
    Written some time before 1985, perhaps much earlier.

I have called . . .
    Written probably in the late 1980s in Berkeley, California.

California is not London
    Written August 3, 1989 in Berkeley, California.

Hope—a diptych
    Left side written sometime before 1985.
    Right side written sometime after that.

Monday Night at the Observatory
    Written in Cedar City, Utah January 15, 1990.

If we were all birds . . .
    Written for a class on appreciating poems and stories
    I taught at the middle school in Cedar City, Utah, 1992.

Five poems in the style of the Chinese
> Written at Dogshine, New Mexico, 2018 in the style of
> Chinese poems as quoted in my "Language and the World".

Stories

Jewish Dogs
> Written in 1980 in Ames, Iowa as a wedding present for friends.

Youth
> Written in 2013 at Dogshine, New Mexico and revised a little after that.

Arfito to Uschi
> The history of this is given in the text.

Devil's Dictionary—an update
> This update of Ambrose Bierce's *The Devil's Dictionary* was written in June, 2020.

Shakespeare and dogs
> The history of this is given in the text.

Plays

The Hanging Tree
> Written for an acting class at The Actors School in Albany, California (next to Berkeley), 1971. Never performed.

Princess
> Written in Berkeley, California about 1972. Never performed.

Ralph
> Written 1972. First performed in Wellington, New Zealand at a theater competition, then at Unity Theater in Wellington in 1977 as part of *Dogalogues or Pinning a Moral Tale on Life*, which I also performed in Berkeley, California, 1984.

My Fight with the Alligators
> Written in Wellington, New Zealand 1976. Performed as a staged reading by Upstart Stage at La Val's Subterranean Cabaret in Berkeley, California, July 19, 1989.

Spiridon
> First half written in 1972 in Berkeley. Finished in 1976 in Wellington, New Zealand. Performed there at Wellington Teachers College and again at Unity Theater.

Essays on logic and . . .

Three Questions about Logic
    Written 2008 at Dogshine, New Mexico. Revised, July, 2022 at Doggy Lodge, New Mexico. Never submitted for publication.

Is There a Problem with Formal Semantics for Natural Languages?
    First written as a query to Jeffrey Pelletier in 2014. Though we had corresponded previously, he never replied. Revised and submitted to *Language under Discussion* in 2022. It was accepted subject to revising. After four rewrites for the editors it was still found to be unacceptable.

Mechanical ≠ Computable
    Written sometime before November, 2007, expanding on work in *Computability*.

Intentions
    Written in July, 2022, revised slightly thereafter.

Numbers
    Written in May–June, 2023.

The Twenty-First or "Lost" Sophism on Self-Reference of John Buridan
    Written sometime before November, 1987. Revised slightly since.

The Procrastination Paradox
    Written in February, 2023 from a discussion with Eduardo "Eddie" Ribeiro and Juan Francisco "Pancho" Rizzo. I planned to revise it to include the advice paradox ("The only advice I can give you is don't take my advice") but I never got around to it.

Addiction studies

Teaching Addicts

From May, 2016 to April 2017 I taught inmates at the Socorro County Detention Center (jail). Almost all of them were, by their own admission, drug addicts or alcoholics. In addition, some were mentally ill. Here I'll describe what I did, why I think it was helpful to the inmates, and how it compares to other work with addicts and those who are suffering.

Teaching critical thinking
I started by distributing copies of my big textbook *Critical Thinking*, going over some of the material and then asking the inmates to read the chapter and do exercises back in their pod (cell block). That didn't work: they didn't have the habit of reading and doing homework on their own, though they certainly had the time.

So I switched to using my smaller textbook *The Pocket Guide to Critical Thinking*. It gives the basic ideas of the larger text but with fewer examples and no exercises. Each chapter is short, and most can be covered in one class of 45 minutes. I would explain the material bit by bit, going around the room asking the inmates to read parts. This made them pay attention to those parts, involved them in the class, and encouraged them to read out loud. Some struggled with reading, and I encouraged them to work together in the pod, helping each other. Then I would distribute exercises that we would do in class, each inmate in turn reading an exercise and all contributing to answering it.

Many inmates liked this. I judged this not just because they returned for class, since any diversion from the horribly boring routine of jail was welcome to them. Rather, more than a few were excited that they could begin to think clearly, to reason, to reflect on what they and others believe. They found that they are not stupid.

The Pocket Guide to Critical Thinking and the exercises present a collection of skills, building one on another. The rigor of the book is crucial. Other texts encourage students to "listen carefully," to "respect the other person," and "to interpret what the other person says charitably." Those are hopeless as guides for how to reason well. They are consequences of learning critical thinking, not the basis of critical thinking, and leave students groping for rules and feeling that they have to be a "good person" to think clearly.

Choices

When I first started, and often since, I was told by people who were sympathetic to the inmates and wanted to encourage me:

They aren't bad people, they just made bad decisions.

This was always said in a sympathetic tone. But it's the basis on which to blame the addicts. They had a choice. They didn't have to end up in jail. Now they must pay. There is no empathy for their suffering; it's justice.

But it's wrong. They didn't make bad decisions. They didn't make any decisions. Asked in exasperation "But what were you thinking?" the only truthful answer they can give is "I wasn't thinking."

Rarely do addicts have a choice. They know no other way. The choice is often to face the horrors and kill yourself or to take a drug, to take many drugs to blot out all, to forget and to feel good—if only for a little while. Until they can't stop taking the drug, not to feel good but not to feel bad from the withdrawal. If you blame them for their addiction, then you have never suffered, you have never felt so bad that another day is impossible. Drugs are not the problem for them—they're the solution. Punishment and threats are nothing to them. It can't be worse than how they feel when there is no drug. We must offer better.

But they had the choice not to start. Yes, when they were eighteen or twenty, or even twelve they experimented, just as you and I took a beer, or cadged a cigarette, or smoked a joint, or even snorted a little. We didn't get hooked; they did. I took morphine for three days when I had surgery and then I stopped, with a day of unpleasant side-effects. If I'd taken it for a week, I'm sure I would have stopped. Others take morphine for a week for a bad back, and they're addicted. Blaming someone for having bad brain chemistry is irrelevant if not wrong.

Besides, how often do we make choices? Did you make a choice to eat another potato chip from the bag lying open on the table? Did you make a choice to drink the beer someone handed you at a party? Did you make a choice to drive the usual way home? Habit guides us, for life would be impossible if we tried to think through every action. We'd be paralyzed. Yet sometimes we need to stop and make a choice. Critical thinking helps us make choices for what is important, to learn new habits.

As the inmates learned to think critically, they began to reflect on what they believe and on whether they should believe what someone else says. They learned how to justify their beliefs and revise them as they learn more. These are skills they need in order to make decisions, indeed even to stop and recognize that a decision needs to be made.

Once I said something stupid in class, hoping the students would challenge me. Then I asked them if they believed it. Most said no. One inmate said nothing. So I asked her why she didn't raise her hand. She said, "Because if I did, you'd ask me why I don't believe it." They were learning.

In critical thinking we learn to look for unstated assumptions. Why do you believe this? Why do I believe this? That is what we need to make choices and to find the basis of our bad habits.

Making good decisions

Critical thinking gives them the skills to make decisions. But that's not enough to make good decisions. For that, they need good goals, good aims, a good way in life.

So after we finished working through a chapter of *The Pocket Guide to Critical Thinking* I would read to them from *The BARK of DOG*. It tells how dogs teach us unconditional love and cats lead us to suffer. We hear stories (all the stories in it are meant to be read out loud) that show us how to be more like dogs: caring, loving, giving unconditionally. We learn to avoid the terrible cats: Hate, Greed, Vengeance, Lust, Gluttony, Pride, Impatience, Indifference, Sloth, Schadenfreude [taking pleasure in the pain of others], Guilt, and Fear, —for they lead us from being loving to suffering. Yet by suffering we learn to love better—or perhaps at all.

Dogs and cats. A bible for those who don't like religion, as one inmate said. But it is also the way of the earliest Christians, of the Quakers now, of Buddhists who do not worship Buddha but emulate his life of compassion. Faith is not important; it is the doing, the charity, that matters.

These stories of dogs, and cats, and people struggling in the world allow the inmates to compare how they live with a better way. Sometimes we talked after a story. Sometimes they cried during a story. One story is about how the most beautiful of all dogs attaches herself to a man who is crazy from guilt because he killed when his tribe fought another. Though she, the dog, could have had any human, for she was beautiful and famous, she found the greatest good in her life being with this man who suffered, who was the "lowest". And the story tells how he came to be honored, though still crazy, because others could see the good in him through the love she gave him. After I read that, one of the women said, "I want to be like her."

The stories are good to hear again and again. Some inmates had been in the jail so long they'd heard the stories three times and still found them moving.

Opening up
Addicts are often frozen emotionally. They cannot be loving. They can only survive. Despite that, they are kind to one another—until they are overwhelmed by the horrors of their lives or the need for drugs.

As they hear the stories from *The BARK of DOG*, they open up. They begin to talk. But the class is always about teaching: the focus is on the critical thinking material and the stories. The focus is not on them. They are not asked to look inward, though some do when they give examples of how to use critical thinking or when they comment on the stories.

For them to become open again, I have to be open, too. I share with them my ups and downs. I told them once that I was very depressed, terribly, so depressed that I was about ready to start taking drugs. After all, I said, the drugs must be really good if you give up everything—family, friends, children—to take them every day. One of the men joked that he could arrange for me to get the drugs. Another, though, warned me not to take them because I would end up in the jail like him. I told him I'd be careful to take the drugs only at home. But then talking with the women (I taught the men and women separately), one said, "Yeah, they'll make you feel better. But afterwards you'll feel worse." The other women agreed and told me more. I told them that I couldn't face feeling worse. I was convinced by them not to take drugs.

This sounds like a contrived episode. But it wasn't. I truly was depressed. They truly did make me avoid drugs, and they helped me see that I was abusing alcohol. I said that I couldn't be an alcoholic because an alcoholic is someone who drinks more than me. They laughed, recognizing this as a perversion of our work on definitions in critical thinking. But they also recognized themselves in the definition.

To help them at all, I had to be open. I had to be consistent: every Wednesday and Friday afternoon, never missing. I had to be trusted.

I told them that what was said in the class stayed in the class, except for talk of criminal plans. I let them know I cared. But I was never enabling. Not sympathetic, but empathetic. They told me they trusted me because I didn't judge them. I was a volunteer: they knew I wasn't paid to be there.

I was warned by the director of the jail and others there that being open was dangerous. Someday one of the inmates will say I said or did something bad—probably sexual. After all, sex is on their minds a lot. Perhaps they believe their accusations—they interpret what you and I say differently from what we expect. They've lived differently, their brains have been fried, either because of the drugs or because the bad wiring is the cause that makes them take drugs, so they have little impulse control. Or perhaps they strike out, kick at anyone they can, and you or I are closest. Then they feel some power—and the powerlessness is overwhelming to them. Not just the powerlessness of being an inmate, but the powerlessness to stop taking much less wanting drugs or to leave a life with hard people.

A comparison to other methods of helping addicts

All you need is love

A standard way to try to help inmates is to recognize that they, as all of us, want love, unconditional love. So we should try to make them "feel good about themselves." "You are worthy of love," we tell them. Everyone is. You can be loved.

That's a dead end. If you're looking for unconditional love, for complete acceptance to justify yourself, to overcome the rejection by your parents, by an uncle who raped you, by a woman who lied to you, by a father who beat you, by teachers who told you you're stupid, love to overcome the guilt for the wrongs you have done—you'll never get it. Whatever is offered is never enough. It has to be there constantly, perfect, always accepting of you. God as the source of the unconditional love you want gets to be thin sustenance. Why did God let them take my baby away if He loves me unconditionally? Why did God let my boyfriend die if He loves me unconditionally? Why does He keep putting drugs in my way so I can't stop if He loves me unconditionally? Theology, it's all for the best, God works in mysterious ways, does not comfort. They cannot see their way by reasoning to the perfection of God's love. They need love now—large doses of it, unconditional. Yet they expect to be betrayed, so that given good—though not perfect—love, they will test it again and again until it breaks. A lover cannot be a saint; he or she needs love, too.

This idea that all we need is love is summed up in the saying:

No se puede vivir sin amor.

"One cannot live without love." Few realize this is a misquote of the saying of the 16th century monk Luis de Leon:

No se puede vivir sin amar.

"One cannot live without being loving." The first leads to a search for love. The second, in which "amar" is the verb rather than the noun "amor" for "love", opens the path to being loving. We, the addicts and ourselves, need to look outwards, not inwards. We need to learn to be loving, not passive but active in our love.

And we need more than love. We need skills—the skills to think clearly. The road to hell is paved with good intentions.

Face up to your faults
Another way of "treating" addicts is to get them to look inward, to make them face that they are addicts, that they lie and cheat and steal, that they hurt others and themselves. If they can face the truth, it will set them free. Then they can learn to love themselves.

But looking inward is as likely to get them stuck facing how horrible they are. And really, they already know that they lie and cheat and steal and hurt others and themselves. At least they know when they're in the class in jail because then they're free of drugs, sober, and can reflect. Outside, hurt and hurting, they are in denial. Then looking at what they have done and are doing is important.

But only as a first step. Yet too often it's claimed that if you look inward, if you learn to accept yourself, to be compassionate to yourself first, then you can reach out to be loving to others. But to focus inward is to encourage selfishness, egotism, me, me, me. It might lead to being loving to others but is equally likely to get stuck there: me, me, me. That is what many have found in psychoanalysis.

The 12-step program
The 12-step method was begun by Alcoholics Anonymous and is now adopted by other groups such as Narcotics Anonymous. These are religious movements, based on an evangelical Christian conception of a just and merciful God. Addicts are told to admit that they are powerless and give themselves to God who will "remove all these

defects of character" and "our shortcomings." For a Jew, a Muslim, a Buddhist to adopt the 12-step method would be to go against his or her own religion. For an atheist to be guided by it, he or she must first accept God. I could never adopt the 12-step method because it would mean giving up my most basic beliefs and world-view. Perhaps it is easier for addicts because they don't have strongly held beliefs.

This method does not encourage the addict to find the power within to change. Addicts are asked to remember the bad they have done and make amends. But we cannot make amends for past hurts we have done, most especially when we were incapable of making choices at the time we did the wrong. Going back to tell people "I'm sorry" is about you, not about them. We have to learn to look forward, to what we can do. The only way to make real amends is to begin to live a good life. Responsibility comes from power within oneself, not by admitting wrongs but by looking each day to be loving.

The only stated goal of Narcotics Anonymous is abstinence, and that through accepting God. I see the goal as living a good life. Walking that path, which anyone can begin whether committed to giving up drugs or not, will lead the addict to want to give up drugs. Abstinence is not a goal but a means.

Narcotics Anonymous is clear that "There is only one requirement for membership, the desire to stop using." But the hard first step is leading addicts to want to stop. The 12-step method seems more to be directed toward getting addicts out of denial, and if it does that, it's good.

And the support of the group at Narcotics Anonymous meetings is important to many. There the addicts are accepted. They depend on the group, they're encouraged to return and return, sharing their stories. Perhaps this is helpful. Perhaps they do gain some power from this.

Being loving

We can learn to be loving without confronting all our fears, our anxieties, our anger. We help others and feel good by the doing. We might never confront our fears—or perhaps we will because others tell us we are good and we don't believe them, so we try to figure out why we don't believe them. But we might never relieve those deep fears and anger. Indeed, none of us ever will. I never have. But looking outwards, helping others, walking with a loving heart, we can persevere.

It's not "truth" that will set you free from addiction, from fears. It's a better way of living to replace the drugs that will make you feel better. We can become loving so that we don't always have to be running from our fears. It doesn't require great effort. It doesn't require looking at your navel to discover your past traumas—real or imagined. It is just *allowing* yourself to be loving as you were when you were a child.

We should be loving and kind and generous with them to make them feel whole and not isolated. But equally, we do so to be an example. You, too, can act this way; you, too, can help others.

The stories of *The BARK of DOG,* which are not only moving but often funny, offer them a better way, summed up in the Covenant of DOG:

- Be kind.
- Be generous.
- Count not the giving and the taking, but give unconditionally.
- Harm no human.
- Harm no dog.
- Keep from thee hate, greed, vengeance, lust, fear, gluttony, pride, impatience, indifference, sloth, schadenfreude, guilt, and allergy, for these are the way of CAT.
- Put from thee all thought of power save the power of a loving heart.

There is no promise of love. But if we are loving we can feel ourselves in the flow of all, the flow of love. Look outward to others, not inward to blackness. Never ask for anything in return, for then kindness becomes a business negotiation. Giving, wholly, with no thought of return, we can become whole and powerful, for there is no power like the power of a loving heart.

This, I believe, is a better way that they can embrace. Yes, giving without expecting anything in return is hard, a hard way. But it's also the easiest way. You smile at someone at the grocery store, you pet a dog, you help someone who's dropped a package, you call someone who is hurting just to say hello, you're there with them—and then you feel good. Truly, virtue is its own reward.

Giving, loving, not blindly enabling the bad but with strength of mind, clarity, and empathy. This they learn with critical thinking and the stories of *The BARK of DOG.*

Teaching Addicts

* * * * * *

I called this essay "Teaching Addicts." But really it's for all of us.

How many of us are lost in making a decision about buying a car, about a job, about moving, about investing our money? We just do, without reflection. How many of us live with bad habits from beliefs we've never examined? How many of us believe nonsense that a little critical thinking would dispel?

How many of us strive for power as the greatest good—power through money, power through being sexually attractive, power to compel others to our will, power to hurt, power to insulate us from feeling. Fear is the goad to wanting such power rather than the power of a loving heart.

The difference between addicts and us is that the addicts know they need help.

Arf 🐾

Richard L. Epstein (Arf)
Dogshine, New Mexico
August, 2017

Postscript 2019
I've recently written *How to Reason: A Practical Guide*. It's based on *The Pocket Guide to Critical Thinking* but with shorter chapters, more summaries and introductions, and exercises for readers to test their skills. I hope to use it to teach inmates. And I hope it will be useful to folks who aren't students but who want to learn how to reason well.

Evaluating Treatments for Addiction

Introduction
- We need to help people with addictions, both for their sake and ours.
- Many ways to treat addicts have been proposed and implemented.
- Addicts who need help, administrators who allocate money for programs, judges who assign inmates to programs, health professionals deciding which programs to offer, and people who want to direct a family member or friend for treatment need to know which programs are best.
- We need clear standards for how to evaluate treatments for addiction.

Here I will set out the basic ideas about what we can and should do in evaluating treatment programs for addiction. I will focus principally on evaluating programs that treat addicts individually, though I will consider in contrast programs that are meant to deal with addiction in a more general way, such as a tax on tobacco.

Most evaluations use and indeed are expected to use numerical analyses of data collected for the programs. Here I will focus on the key ideas about what constitutes a good/useful/convincing evaluation, since those must be understood before any data is collected much less analyzed numerically. Only in the last sections will I make suggestions about what programs might be effective.

Objective versus subjective
Objective criteria for evaluating addiction programs is considered superior to subjective criteria, especially if the objective data is given numerically. But what is meant by "objective"?

> A claim is *subjective* if whether it is true or whether it is false depends on what someone, or some thing, or some group of people thinks, believes, or feels. A claim that is not subjective is *objective*.

For example, the following is subjective:
(1) Heroin addicts prefer heroin to food and shelter.

It's about what heroin addicts think, believe, or feel. The following is objective:

(2) Someone who has been injecting heroin two times per day for one month and has not had heroin for two days, and has not eaten for two days, and has no place to sleep, and who has no money, if given $100 will spend it on heroin.

It may seem clear that the subjective claim (1) follows from the objective claim (2). But *no subjective claim follows from only objective claims*. No observations about what a person does can lead to a claim about what that person thinks, believes or feels without some assumption about how behavior links to thoughts. In this case we can use:

(3) If someone has no place to sleep and no food and spends his or her money on heroin, that person prefers heroin to food or shelter.

That seems obvious. But in many cases when we try to formulate the link between the objective claims and the subjective conclusion, we find that we have to make a substantial assumption that is not obvious.

We classify *criteria of evaluation as subjective* if they contain even one subjective claim. Otherwise, the criteria are *objective*. It would seem that objective criteria are always superior to subjective ones, for what is objective, it's thought, is clear and precise and not subject to judgment. But often considerable judgment is needed to interpret numerical data. And often subjective claims require no judgment to evaluate. For example, almost everyone agrees that the subjective claim "It is wrong to torture puppies" is true. We have no difficulty in adopting it as a standard for enacting a law about humane treatment of animals. When (almost) all of us agree that a subjective claim such as this one about puppies or (3) is true, we say the claim is *intersubjective*. Intersubjective claims can be as useful as objective claims in evaluating whether a treatment program is effective.

Definitions of "addiction" and "addict"

Here are some definitions from sources concerned with treating addiction.

> Addiction is a primary, chronic disease of brain reward, motivation, memory and related circuitry. Dysfunction in these circuits leads to characteristic biological, psychological, social and spiritual manifestations. This is reflected in an individual pathologically

pursuing reward and/or relief by substance use and other behaviors. Addiction is characterized by inability to consistently abstain, impairment in behavioral control, craving, diminished recognition of significant problems with one's behaviors and interpersonal relationships, and a dysfunctional emotional response. Like other chronic diseases, addiction often involves cycles of relapse and remission. Without treatment or engagement in recovery activities, addiction is progressive and can result in disability or premature death. American Society of Addiction Medicine

Addiction is a complex condition, a brain disease that is manifested by compulsive substance use despite harmful consequence. People with addiction (severe substance use disorder) have an intense focus on using a certain substance(s), such as alcohol or drugs, to the point that it takes over their life. American Psychiatric Association

The definition of addiction is explored. Elements of addiction derived from a literature search that uncovered 52 studies include: (a) engagement in the behavior to achieve appetitive effects, (b) preoccupation with the behavior, (c) temporary satiation, (d) loss of control, and (e) suffering negative consequences. Differences from compulsions are suggested. While there is some debate on what is intended by the elements of addictive behavior, we conclude that these five constituents provide a reasonable understanding of what is intended by the concept. Conceptual challenges for future research are mentioned.

"Considering the Definition of Addiction"
Steve Sussman and Alan N. Sussman,
International Journal of Environmental Research and Public Health, vol. 8, October 2011, pp. 4025–4038

Addiction is any repeated behavior, substance-related or not, in which a person feels compelled to persist, regardless of its negative impact on his life and the lives of others. Addiction involves:
1. compulsive engagement with the behavior, a preoccupation with it;
2. impaired control over the behavior;
3. the persistence or relapse despite evidence of harm; and
4. dissatisfaction, irritability, or intense craving when the object—be it a drug, activity, or other goal—is not immediately available.

Gabor Maté , *In the Realm of Hungry Ghosts,* pp. 136–137

To classify a person as an addict by any one of these definitions involves subjective criteria: the person has "a craving"; "diminished recognition of significant problems"; "intense focus"; "preoccupation with the behavior"; "temporary satiation"; "dissatisfaction, irritability". A drug counselor, a judge, a jail administrator, a researcher, anyone who classifies a person as an addict by any of these definitions must draw a conclusion from the person's behavior to the person's thoughts, feelings, or beliefs. Still, most of us would agree in most cases whether the criteria apply. So in use these criteria are usually intersubjective.

Invoking what counts as a "harmful consequence" or "negative impact" is also a subjective standard. Usually most of us agree on our classifications of outcomes as good or bad. But the group of people whose agreement is invoked often excludes addicts themselves. We would classify death by an overdose of drugs as a negative consequence, yet I have met addicts who say that it is a welcome consequence, though not one they actively seek. We would classify buying and injecting drugs of unknown origin and purity as a bad consequence of addiction, whereas an addict might classify that as a good outcome for the need she has.

Since any criteria to evaluate whether a program for treating addicts is effective must involve a definition of "addict" or "addiction", the criteria must be subjective.

There is no way to avoid a subjective basis for any study of addiction.

That does not mean that every conclusion about the effectiveness of a program is just personal opinion. What is subjective are claims about what a purported addict thinks, believes, or feels, or what we think is a good outcome. We have every right to demand that:

- In a study of addiction the subjective claims on which the conclusions are based are generally agreed to be true.
- Whenever possible, claims about behavior are used in place of subjective claims.
- The evaluation makes explicit the claims linking those objective claims to the subjective ones in the standards and conclusion.

In this way, we can hope to have confidence in an evaluation as intersubjective.

What do we mean when we judge a program to be effective or successful?

There are two kinds of standards.

What the program says is its goal
Whether it is effective means whether or to what extent it accomplishes that goal. This is the *internal standard* for judging a program.

Our standards
Whether a program is effective means whether it achieves a goal or goals that we consider important. This is an *external standard* for judging a program.

For example, suppose your neighbor wants to make a chair. He works at it in his garage. He makes a chair. He has been successful by his internal standard. But the chair is so ugly and rickety that only he will want to use it. From outside, we'd say he should have made a good chair, one that most folks would recognize as a chair and be willing to use. By our external standards he was not successful. Are we justified in substituting our goals for his? Yes, if we are paying him.

Internal standards
Let's first consider internal standards for judging a treatment program.

Right away we can say that if a program has no clear goal, then there is no way to judge whether it is effective on its own terms.

For example, suppose a program says that its purpose is to cure addicts. We can't judge whether it is effective because that's too vague. What counts as a cure? Completely abstaining from the addiction—whether that's heroin, meth, gambling, or video games? But an addict can substitute one addiction for another. So perhaps a cure means that the person abstains from all addictive behavior. For a year? For six months? Forever? Or perhaps a cure means not complete abstinence but only reducing the frequency of yielding to the addiction. And how many people who are treated by the program should be cured? One half? One tenth? All?

If a program has a vague standard, then any result can be counted as a success by interpreting the standard in the way that the outcome supports. For example, suppose a program has the standard of curing addicts, not being clearer than that. After a couple years, it turns out that half of the people who participated stayed away from the addiction for one month after the end of the program. That's what we got, and that's pretty good, the program managers would say; we've been successful. But that's not what they set out to do. It's easy to keep the standard vague and then the program can say it's effective no matter how little or much it does because what it does is what's counted as accomplishing the goal.

If a very clear goal of a program is not given in advance, there is no way to judge the program. There is no direction at all for the program. The program is not worth our time to consider, much less to evaluate.

Some programs do have clear goals. For example, a state legislature institutes a new tax on tobacco with the goal of reducing the number of chronic smokers. That is a standard we can hope to evaluate, perhaps by interviewing people about how much they smoke and seeing whether tobacco sales have gone down. Or a big city sets up a needle exchange program with the goal of reducing cases of HIV and hepatitis. That is clear, and we might try to evaluate it by looking at how many cases of HIV and hepatitis are reported by doctors and hospitals.

To say that the goal of a treatment program must be clear does not mean that there must be an objective, numerical way to decide if the goal is met. A subjective goal need not be unclear, and some subjective goals are very clear. For example, to educate addicts about the risks of injecting drugs is a clear goal. Perhaps some numerical data could be collected from testing, but the link between that data and the subjective conclusion that the program helped addicts understand will be suspect. Other ways, perhaps evaluation by teachers and students, are needed and are not less reliable for not being objective and numerical.

Someone might object that to set up clear goals is to narrow the program. We'll do whatever we can and hope to accomplish something. But without a clear goal there is no direction, no idea of what the treatment or methods are meant to accomplish, and that alone justifies evaluating the program as ineffective. Besides, the goal need not be narrow: it could be to get at least 50% of all participants to give up all addictions for at least two years after the end of the program. But it's doubtful that a program would adopt that as a goal because it's so difficult to accomplish. To require clear goals forces program managers to become clear about what they think they really can accomplish, which often leads to more "modest" goals.

External standards
External standards, the goals a treatment program should have, may be established by a consensus among health professionals, or by legislation, or by some other means.

For example, it may take many years to come to a consensus that, say, getting a person to give up one addiction is not enough: the goal should be to get a person to give up all addictive behavior, not trading one addiction for another.

There is a large debate now about whether it is a good goal to try to get an addict to reduce how often he or she uses the drug, or gambles, or plays video games, so that the person can function in society. Part of that debate has to be about what is meant by "function in society." If that can be made clear and that goal is adopted, a physician or legislator might say that a program which sets out to do that has an acceptable goal. Someone who disagrees and believes that only complete abstinence is an acceptable goal would consider a program to reduce harm as ineffective on the face of it. These debates depend on our subjective criteria for what counts as good or bad. But data can be important. If it can be shown that no treatment program gets even a substantial proportion of those it treats to give up all addiction, then as certain as some people may be that this is the only good goal, perhaps they will be willing to accept a "lesser" goal of reducing harm. Good arguments are essential, and basing those on good data can help.

Helping all compared to helping some
A broad division in goals of programs for addiction is whether they are intended to help particular individuals or to help society.

For example, if the goal is to help society, then putting all addicts in jail would seem to be a good solution to reducing the harm they do to "the rest of us." But it is not a good program for helping addicts.

A needle exchange program, offering addicts a clean needle in return for a used one, might have as a goal to help addicts not get sick or die. But equally, it could have the goal of helping society as a whole by reducing the incidence of HIV and hepatitis in the community, since an addict can pass those diseases to others.

Any evaluation must be clear about which of these kinds of goals is invoked for judgment.

Other factors in evaluating treatment programs

Risk

Judging a program by its internal standards can miss what bad might come from it.

For example, putting addicts in jail for the goal of reducing crime might be effective by that standard. But it has the potential, indeed almost certain harm of making more addicts criminals: they learn how to rob and steal, which they have to when they get out because they can't get a job. That program also has the harm of passing on hepatitis, HIV, and other diseases to both the addicts and others in jail, so that when inmates get out they pass those diseases to others.

Or a program could treat addicts "naturally" by requiring them to give up all drugs, including medically prescribed ones for depression, with the goal of getting the addicts to give up their addictions permanently. That might "cure" some addicts, but it could also lead to more suicides.

Or a needle exchange program could result in lots of needles being thrown away in the neighborhood, with children picking them up and getting infected.

It should be possible to conjecture what risks might follow from a program and then see if those follow. It should also be possible to see if other risks, unforeseen, have followed from implementation of a program.

Cost—and relative worth

How much a program costs and what programs are competing with it for funds are important in evaluating programs.

For example, suppose one program has the goal to keep addicts away from addiction for two years. It's somewhat successful: say 10% of the participants "stay clean" that long. Another program has the goal to reduce the harm that addicts do to themselves, keeping them healthy, and to reduce the harm that addicts do to others, keeping them from committing crimes. It is pretty successful: say, 50% of the people it treats have no new severe infections and are not arrested while in the program. There isn't enough money to support both programs. The first costs a lot per addict, the second cost less than half as much. Which one should an administrator give money to?

Part of an evaluation of a program must be how much it costs for what it accomplishes and how that compares to other programs, both for the good of the goal and the cost. Such an evaluation depends on what subjective criteria are adopted for the relative worth of programs. No numbers alone can decide that.

Means
Suppose a program has as goal to reduce and eventually eliminate all heroin addiction in this country. And it's pretty clear it will be effective. And it won't cost much. Should we support it?

The program will accomplish its goals by distributing heroin mixed with fentanyl in packets that look just like ones that are distributed on street corners. Lots of addicts will die. Others will stop taking heroin for fear of dying, and those that continue will eventually die.*

We reject the program because we reject the means: the ends do not justify the means. That's not because of the possible harm: many people reckon that an addict dying is a positive consequence not a negative one. No, we reject it because most of us believe that it's immoral, unethical, just plain wrong to kill people.

Is the program good?
In summary, the evaluation of a treatment program involves judging:
- Whether the program is effective by its internal standards.
- Whether the program is effective by our external standards.
- What possible harm can come from the program.
- How much the program costs.
- The value of the program in comparison with other programs.
- Whether its means are acceptable

No one of these by itself is sufficient.

In the end we are evaluating whether the program is *good*, whether it passes our criteria for what counts as good. That will involve moral, ethical, and political judgment. *Thinking that objective numerical data can determine an evaluation is itself a moral judgment: what people think, believe, or feel is not important.*

In what follows I will focus primarily on the first two points: how we can or should judge the effectiveness of a treatment program. The

---

* If this seems far-fetched, consider that in the Philippines President Duterte had the explicit goal of killing all addicts, and he was supported by a significant portion of the population there.

20   *Evaluating Treatments for Addiction*

discussion will be, as it has been so far, about the principles and methods involved.

Cause and effect
Particular causal claims
To claim that a program is effective, by any standard, is to make a claim about cause and effect. This program caused this result. So we must be clear about how to reason about cause and effect.

Suppose a treatment program says that it's had success with this person: she was addicted to heroin and meth and now no longer takes any illegal drugs. That's a claim about cause and effect: "This person was addicted and entered the program caused this person to no longer take illegal drugs." How can we tell if this is true? After all, it could be just coincidence, or the addict gave up drugs despite being in the program. Here are the standard steps in deciding whether a cause-and-effect claim is true, illustrated with this example.*

- *The cause happened.*

We can describe the cause with the claim "The person was addicted to heroin and meth and participated in the program." It's clear that's true.

- *The effect happened.*

We can describe the effect with the claim "The person no longer takes any illegal drugs." We can check that—if the addict is willing to be tested and responds truthfully to questions. That's a pretty big "if", but let's suppose it's been done and the claim is true.

- *The cause precedes the effect.* This isn't so clear. Perhaps the person quit using illegal drugs before entering the program. She felt that she needed the drugs, but she hadn't taken any for some time before entering the program. This is often the case with an inmate assigned to a program who has been kept from drugs by being in jail.

- *It is nearly impossible for the cause to happen and the effect not to happen.*

This has to be checked against some obvious assumptions we make but don't normally state, like "The person had a choice whether to take drugs." This condition looks to be hard to verify because there are always many people in a treatment program who do not give up drugs.

---

* The analysis of cause and effect here follows the textbook presentation in my *Critical Thinking*, 5th edition.

- *The cause makes a difference—if the cause had not happened, the effect would not have happened.*
This is even more difficult to verify. Some people stop taking drugs on their own, regardless of whether they are in a program.
- *There is no common cause.*
This, too, is difficult to verify. Perhaps the person decided that she would give up drugs, and after that decision entered the program. In that case, the decision would have caused both the addict to quit and to participate in the program. Or the person was in jail and entered the program just because it was less awful than being in jail, and being in jail is what caused the person to enter the program and to quit taking drugs.

These are the steps we have to make in evaluating any *particular* causal claim: this happened because of that. One person, one "outcome". The problems in doing so, illustrated in this example, make it hard if not impossible to verify any cause-and-effect claim about the success of treating a particular addict. There is too much to consider in each step of the evaluation that we can't know: the person's beliefs, the person's desires, the physical constitution of the person, how much the family supported the addict—the list could go on. Typically we cannot disentangle one of these as being a cause or even part of the cause of the addict being "cured" or "helped" as opposed to participation in the program being the cause.

Above all, there is the difficulty of ascertaining some of the motives, thoughts, beliefs, feelings, and desires of the person who is said to have been cured by the program. Even if the addict is certain the program helped or "cured" him, there is no reason to think it did. Perhaps he was just ready to quit. It's a standard mistake in evaluating causal claims to claim that because this happened after, therefore it was because of. We don't need a psychologist to tell us that often we can't discern why we do what we do, what motivates us. We know this every day if we think a bit, realizing that the rationale we gave for taking the second donut ("I didn't want it to go to waste") was far from the basic craving for sweets this morning that made us eat it.

But what if lots of people who entered the program gave up taking illegal drugs? Surely that's evidence that the program is successful. That's no evidence if all that's claimed is that each of those people was "cured" by the program, for lots of doubtful particular causal claims don't add up to a good general one. What's needed is a different way to evaluate the evidence that lots of people who entered the treatment program gave up taking illegal drugs.

Cause-in-population claims
Suppose a program has the goal of getting the addicts who enter the program to quit all addictions for 6 months after the program is over. And suppose that lots of those who participate in the program do quit, say 40%. To say that therefore the program is successful is to make a cause-and-effect claim, but not necessarily one about each addict individually. Rather, it would be to claim that participating in the program is *a* cause, a part of what led the addicts to give up their addiction. If we can show that very few addicts who didn't participate in the program gave up all addictions, say only 8%, we have some evidence that the program is a significant part of the addicts quitting.

But addicts who don't participate in this program might be in other treatments, or in jail, or at home with family who are trying to get them to stop. A definitive study would be to compare addicts who enter the program to ones who have no treatment, no help at all, and are not forced to refrain from the addiction because they're in prison. But we can't do that because it's unethical to withhold treatment. We can't have a *control group* for comparison that goes for the length of the study.

Nor can we look at all people who quit and note that very few did not participate in the program. No program treats enough people to make such a study possible. That is, we can't do an *uncontrolled effect-to-cause experiment*.

Our only hope for establishing that the link between participating in the program and quitting is somehow causal is to compare addicts who participate in the program to addicts who do not participate and see if more who are in the program quit. This would be an *uncontrolled cause-to-effect study*. The problem with this is to find other addicts who do not participate in the program. Perhaps you could look at people who are in other treatment programs or in jail or prison. But then at most you can compare the rates at which addicts quit their addiction for various programs. But another program may have a different goal, so we'd have an apples-and-oranges comparison. We could try to compare addicts who enter the program with addicts who have no treatment and are not in jail or prison. That's very difficult because the main way to find addicts is to go to programs like needle exchanges or food kitchens and try to interview them. There's no reason to think those people are representative of all addicts who aren't in the program, and anyway, even providing food is a treatment: perhaps just being healthier and knowing that people care can help an addict quit. You could go up to people on the street who look like addicts and ask them if they are addicts, but besides being dangerous there's no reason to think they're representative of addicts who aren't in the program, for there are lots of addicts who more or less function and have homes and jobs.

There doesn't seem to be any way to do a cause-and-effect study that could reliably show a link between being in the program and quitting all addictions. Yet it sure looks like the program is successful. How can we justify that claim?

We study as best we can other groups of addicts: ones in other treatment programs, however minimal; ones in prisons; ones we can find on the street or elsewhere. If we can say that few of those quit all addictions for six months—we can't say anything useful. It's apples and oranges again.

So we look for other factors that might be significant for leading addicts to quit: previous decision to quit; family support; health; level of education; gender; age; employment; color of hair; number of times the person has been in a treatment program; . . . . We look at only addicts who participate in the program. If we have some evidence about how likely it is that someone with a certain level of education is likely to quit; how likely it is that someone who has family support—however that is defined—is likely to quit; how likely it is that a man is likely to quit; that a woman is likely to quit; that a transgender person is likely to quit; . . . then we can compare those rates to the rate at which participants in the program quit. We can "factor out" those other possible causes. But this we can't do. We can't find those groups, and even if we can find a lot of addicts for each of those characteristics, there's no reason to think that we can get reliable information from them. Many may refuse to answer or will answer falsely, either exaggerating their drug use to snub their nose at the interviewer or minimizing their drug use to please the interviewer.

All we are left with is the raw number that this percentage of addicts who entered the program quit. We compare that to other programs that are meant to have the same goal. Can we then say that the program that has the best "success rate" is best? No, for they might start with very different groups of addicts: some may be private treatment programs for only the wealthy; others may deal principally or only with released convicts. And to factor out those differences would require a study of those groups, which we just saw is extremely difficult if not impossible.

Why not run the treatment program with lots of different groups: wealthy, convicts, inmates, ... If we get the same result for all of them, then it seems that the program matters. But if we don't, that shows nothing because perhaps the people who run the program treat wealthy people differently from poor convicted felons. Or we could try to run the program with mixed groups of addicts. Then if we get a high percentage quitting, we could say with more confidence that if you take this program, there's that percentage chance that you'll stop quitting. That's about the best that I can see. But though it's said to be the "same" program, all that means is that the person running it has an outline, directions for how to lead the program, and different leaders may do the program very differently. It may be the particular leader who matters more than the program.

It seems that the best we can do is say that if the program is run time and again and the percentage of those who quit is more or less consistently X%, then if you are like the other participants in this program and you participate in the treatment program, there's an X% chance that you'll quit your addiction. We can't do any reliable cause-and-effect study to show that the program is even a factor much less the main factor in getting people to quit. We are inclined to interpret the percentage as indicating a causal link, but we are not justified in doing so.

Yet even this cannot be done, for we don't know what "like the other people in the program" means. That's a generalization. We know what the sample is: the people in the program. But what is the population? To generalize you have to specify the population in advance. Otherwise, it's just mining data. The sample isn't representative of any population other than itself, and it certainly wasn't chosen randomly. Yet there is a great tendency to want to use the data to predict. To predict what? Given any group of people who resemble the ones in the program, if they take the program there's an 18.5% chance that they will stop taking all illegal drugs for 6 months? But we're not justified in this. First, what are the relevant factors that determine what the population is. Desire to quit? Height? Weight? Gender? Age? Race? Criminal history? We can't find the population from the sample. And if we do specify the population in advance, there's no way to ensure that the people in the program are a representative sample. I don't see any way to get a good generalization that could lead to predictions. If we could get a good generalization, then we could use it to establish a cause-in-population claim.

* * * * * * * * * *

There is much more to do to complete this essay. Published articles that evaluate treatment programs should be examined in the light of the issues raised here. Discussions with people running programs and administrators to see what concerns they have and what standards they use in evaluating programs need to be done.

That is a lot of work, which I cannot do without funding.

My guess is that the conclusion of this essay will be that qualitative rather than quantitative evaluations are what we should be using, along with very careful statements of what we consider to be good or bad goals, methods, etc. That would need to be made clear in what count as suitable or good methods for making such subjective (qualitative) judgments.

I suspect that a review of the literature will show that no personal treatment program will have a substantially greater "success" in getting addicts to quit than doing nothing, since a percentage of addicts quit each year on their own. But this I have to verify. If so, it would seem that the goal of a treatment program should be to help addicts make the decision to quit, supporting them by keeping them healthy, and ensuring that after the program they have support to continue in their goal.

Richard L. "Arf" Epstein
Advanced Reasoning Forum
P. O. Box 635, Socorro, NM 87801
(575) 835-2517
rle@AdvancedReasoningForum.org

Richard L. Epstein has a Ph.D. in mathematics from the University of California, Berkeley. He was a Fulbright Fellow to Brazil and a National Academy of Sciences Visiting Scholar to the Polish Academy of Sciences. He has written four research books on evaluating evidence: *The Fundamentals of Argument Analysis*, *Prescriptive Reasoning*, *Reasoning in Science and Mathematics*, and *Cause and Effect, Conditionals, Explanations*. He has made that research accessible to students in his textbooks *Critical Thinking*, 5th edition with Michael Rooney and *How to Reason + Reasoning in the Sciences*.

IN THE BODY

– TOO GOOD IS JUST AWFUL

(the circles are meant to be cartoons)

This is a draft of a comic book to help you understand how addiction works in the body. You'll see the similarity of many kinds of addiction, what is common to them, how and why we're susceptible to them, and what repair of them means. The focus is on the "mechanics" of addiction in the body and why it's so hard to break free of addictions.

Descriptions of cartoons are in italics.

What is described as a **node** is meant to be like a little light bulb on a stalk to be printed in yellow.

The rest of the book is meant to be in black and white.

Also planned but not written:

The Road to Addiction
Archetypal stories of people who have become addicted.
How they became addicted.
The effects of their addiction on themselves.
The effects of their addiction on their family and friends.
The effects of their addiction on the rest of us.

Helping Addicts—Helping Ourselves
A survey of the main methods of "treating" addicts.

Names, characters, and incidents relating to any of the characters in this text are used fictitiously, and any resemblance to actual persons, living or dead, is entirely coincidental. *Honi soit qui mal y pense.*

WHAT IS ADDICTION ?

WHAT'S GOING ON IN OUR BODIES ?

Our bodies, our brains want what is GOOD and try to avoid what is BAD.

Addiction is when the GOOD becomes BAD.

> *Someone shooting up heroin, happy for a moment, then croaking. Dog sniffing at the body—howling: what happened to my master?*

TOO GOOD IS JUST AWFUL!

*   *   *   *   *   *

Back with the first humans, some survived and had children. Others died young or didn't have children. We've evolved to survive.

> *On the African plains. Roaming.*

MEAT! GOOD!
The ones who ate meat got more protein and more energy than those who ate only fruit and greens. They lived longer. Their children survived.

> *Gathered around a dead beast, eating the meat.*

COOKING—Meat and Fat! GOOD
Some figured out how to control and use fire. They cooked their meat.
 GOOD!

> *Cooking meat on an open fire. Fat dripping.*

They survived better: they could digest the meat more easily, getting more out of it. They could eat the fat, which helped them store energy for lean times. The ones who liked meat and fat survived.

> *Brain. Wiring, an arrow labeled "meat" points to one part where a few nodes light up. Next to it a part that's labeled "fat" and a few nodes light up. Also tongue and nose lighting up for taste and smell.*

Their brains signaled what was good to them—they didn't have to make a choice. They passed on that kind of brain wiring to their children. And they survived better.

Mama and baby, cut away of skull to show brain of each. Baby has small nodes ready to light up for meat and fat.

SWEETS! Fruit. GOOD!
Eating fruit helped them survive.
Vitamins, minerals, instant sugar energy really helped.

Eating fruit. Moving camp, some sluggish. Eat berries and get energy and work better and they move, eating berries as they go.

Some with scurvy, eat lemons and potatoes and get well.

The brains of those who liked fruit signaled GOOD.
And those humans passed on that kind of brain to their children.

Brain. Wiring, with nodes lighting up as eating fruit. Area labeled "sweet".

SALT! GOOD!
It's needed to survive. All of us have come to want it.

Eating salt. A few nodes in "salt" area light up.

EATING A LOT when there was meat or fat or sugar helped them survive. They were ready for the lean times.

Eating a lot. Brains continue to light up. They get fatter. Then lean times. Fat ones surviving, lean ones dying.

Too much fat, too much meat, too much sugar, too much salt— *not a problem.* There just wasn't that much they could get.

*   *   *   *   *

RUNNING!
Being healthy. People who ran a lot got strong, survived, could escape or catch food. They felt fit. GOOD!

THRILLS! Escape! GOOD!
Danger avoided. They had to take risks for hunting, finding a new place to live.

Running to chase a deer. Running to escape a bear up a tree. Then looking healthy. Nodes light up in center for "feeling fit". Another part labeled "thrills" lights up.

*   *   *   *   *

Addiction in the Body 31

JOB WELL DONE!
It feels great to work and get praise.

> *Woman and man making a shelter. Others praise them.*
> *Standing back, feeling good.*

People who could work to a goal survived better.
Satisfaction was the reward.

> *Brain center for "job well done"—nodes light up spelling*
> *"satisfaction".*

*   *   *   *   *

We have lots of centers and nodes that light up when there's GOOD.

> *Show lots of wiring and nodes ready but not lit up in*
> *"centers", which are labeled: salt, sugar, meat, fat, thrills,*
> *healthy, satisfaction.*

We don't choose to have them. We're born with them. Or we're born with some and others develop as we grow as children. Some centers get really big.

> *Child eating too much. Brain center for eating fat and sugar*
> *gets way more nodes—compare to other child's brain.*

> *Child getting thrills, taught by parent.*
> *Thrill center gets lots more nodes.*

Or we get parts that don't develop much because of how we're raised.

> *Parent teaching child that meat and fat is bad.*
> *That center shrinks.*

> *Parent is fearful and lazy, child emulates, center for thrills*
> *and fitness doesn't develop.*

And some are born with or develop a center that's way too big. They're less likely to survive.

> *Thrill center too big, picking up rattlesnake, bitten, dies.*

*   *   *   *   *

Avoiding what is BAD was also crucial for surviving.

> *Eating a berry, makes person sick. Try again because tastes*
> *so good but stop. Avoid. BAD.*

Ones who developed a control center that said STOP survived better.

Brain, lighting up for berries, control center putting up a STOP sign. Shuts down the nodes that were lighting up.

The control center is almost not there when we're small—we're all just impulse.

Small child wanting candy, mama says no, child cries.

As we get older, it grows.

Child admonished, learns to wait.
Dog taught to sit before getting treat.
(asterisk: That's why we treat children differently in the law.)

The control center didn't develop to stop eating, or running, or working except when those made you sick or interfere with living—you could feel it was BAD and you stopped.

*　　*　　*　　*　　*

Now there's plenty of food. The pleasure centers can't stop lighting up: fat, sugar, salt. The control center is not strong enough to stop it. OBESE.

Eating potato chips, eating from a package labeled "Fried Pork Rinds". Drinking Coca Cola. Stuffing it down at the BBQ. Obese.

More eating, less control—cut away of brain and big centers for salt, sugar, fat while the control center is small.

*　　*　　*　　*　　*

RUNNING

Now it's easy, just put on shoes and go out, not over rocks and through brush and thorns, not to escape. Running feels good: "runner's high". But the high is too good and you can't stop wanting it, even when you should. The control center isn't strong enough.

Brain lights up when running—"endorphins" washing over brain. Runner keeps doing it. 1 mile. 5 miles. 10 miles. Shins hurt. Forgets family. Knees bad. Ankle breaks. Wants to continue. Body breaks down.

Control center of brain small, "fit" center too large.

*　　*　　*　　*　　*

Addiction in the Body 33

THRILLS are now easy and seem safe.

Roller coaster. Horror movie. Sky diving. Bungee jumping.

But some can't stop. Their thrill center has become too strong, their control is too weak.

Car racing in city and crash.

Gambling. Thrill. Brain nodes light up.

    *   *   *   *   *

ACCOMPLISHMENT, feeling good by completing a good project is now SOOOO EASY with a video game. Each little step. "YES! I did it!" Sucked into the dreamland of being great through what you're doing, as if it were real, the center for job well done grows and the control center weakens.

Adult playing video game, clock shows passing of many hours.

    *   *   *   *   *

Some don't develop control centers enough.

Mother spoiling child, then child is adult and wants without thought.

No mother, no father, just growing up on street and no impulse control.

Boy not told to stop hitting his little sister. She hits her little brother. Sassing back to mama. No discipline.

Cut away: control center not developed.

They can't stop wanting to eat, or wanting to run, or wanting thrills, or playing a video game.

Adult continues playing video game (earlier cartoon). Adult ignores baby, continues playing. Baby continues to cry, cough, on floor, crawling toward stove. Adult ignores all.

Obese person eating and eating.

Gambling and not stopping though lover tries to get her to stop.

    *   *   *   *   *

ADDICTION!

Any activity—eating, running, wanting thrills—that lights up the pleasure nodes and can make us feel good can become addictive. We want the pleasure nodes to light up.

Several pictures of the brain with pleasure nodes: in one for salt and fa, in another for sugar, in another for thrills. Some with those nodes more plentiful, over-developed, control center small.

If the control center isn't strong enough, or habit makes your brain grow a lot more nodes in one of those centers, or your brain is wired to want a particular kind of good, you can't stop. Just wanting to feel good, doing it over and over again, that alone makes the control center smaller, weaker, so we can ignore it when it tells us it's BAD and we should STOP.

Someone eating. Pleasure center grows for that, control center gets weak over time. Control center holding up smaller and smaller "STOP" signs, until almost not there.

In brain, control center of an addict—small. Getting smaller with repeating the pleasure activity. In brain center of non-addict, control center bigger. No problem stopping.

*   *   *   *   *

HABIT!
What worked before will work again, so keep doing it. That's good for survival, but out of control in addiction.

(Not really centers. More like wiring and nodes—neurons—that release chemicals that attach to other neurons in a big net that makes that GOOD feeling.)

Wiring net, close up of a neuron. Label "That's science!"

*   *   *   *   *

Some brains don't have enough nodes for pleasure.

Some people are born that way.

Baby with brain with few nodes for pleasure. Baby cries.

Mother drinking alcohol. Baby's brain small with control center so small that need magnifying glass to see it.

Some develop that way.

Baby ignored when crying.

Child hit by parent. Fearful.

Parents always complaining and criticizing.

Parents alway arguing, no love.

That's depression. You can't get the pleasure nodes to light up.

Few nodes in brain for pleasure. All "hiding".
Control center HUGE.

Someone with almost no pleasure nodes—only a few and "out of order" signs on them, and person is preparing to hang self.

People turn to gambling, running, meat-salt-sugar, and video games to overcome the depression.

Gambling, and overcomes the depression—pleasure nodes light up.

But it doesn't work for long. We have to continue doing it. And continue doing it.

Depressed again, and gambling again to get some pleasure nodes lighting up in depression brain. Again, and again.

*   *   *   *   *

DRUGS

Cocaine, heroin, methamphetamine hijack the pleasure nodes.
They light up all the pleasure nodes at once—release all the chemicals.
WOW!

Couple kids, "Let's try it." Taking cocaine.
All the nodes light up.

Couple kids, "Let's try it." Taking meth.
All the nodes light up.

Couple kids, "Let's try it." Taking heroin.
All the nodes light up.

The greatest! EUPHORIA! Overwhelmed!
This never happens normally.

Feeling good vs. euphoria. CHEAP THRILLS!

Someone takes heroin first time, blissful.

Someone takes cocaine first time, super feeling.

Someone takes meth first time, powerful feeling, super capable.

DRUGS! Make you feel better than good—can overcome depression. Even if you're normal, it's SOOO GREAT! And lasts a long time!

> *Taking meth, pleasure nodes still lighting up 8 hours later.*

Until the drug wears off. CRASH! Depression. Can't activate the pleasure nodes cause they're all worn out.

> *Afterwards. All the pleasure centers worn out—*
> *the nodes look pooped, hanging limply on their stalks.*
> *All grey Like a depression brain.*

You want that good feeling again. But also to get over the crash-depression.

> *Looking for drugs desperately. Takes the drug again.*

Yes, some stop after the first try.

> *Conked out. Child tries to revive the person. Finally person gets up, takes child to bathroom. Loving with child, "I can't take care of you if I'm out of it" and passes by the offer of more drugs.*

Why? Their control center is strong enough to resist? They have good goals—like taking care of their child? They're not wired in the brain to want that much—like people who can't eat sugar or can't eat peanuts—and the body just stops you?

> *Getting drunk. Waking up the next morning hung over.*
> *"No more—that's awful."*

Some don't stop after the first try because everyone's doing it.

> *At party offered more, like a beer. Only it's pills.*
> *Why not?*
> *At the street corner with buddies. C'mon, are you chicken?*

And some are hooked right away—the first time, they have to have more.

> *First beer, great! Then another, and another, and another.*
>
> *First meth, great! Then conked out. Child looking on.*
> *Walks right past the child, unaware of it, and hurries out*
> *to find a meth score.*

WHY? The control center isn't strong enough to stop it at the first try?

Addiction in the Body 37

Or the brain is wired badly and just susceptible, like people who can't stop eating sweets? Or they are depressed and it blocks out the bad feeling?

Depressed and cutaway of brain showing that depression. Then taking drugs and black cloud obscured.

Brain with nodes saying "Hit me!" "Hit me again!"

They take the drug again to have that feeling of euphoria, a "HIGH". WOW. Or just to feel normal. Or just to get over the depression.

Taking drug again and thought bubble of black cloud and rain goes away.

Then CRASH! So take more.

Black cloud comes back bigger. Takes more drugs.

2-page spread:
"Before": Man playing with his children at the park, with wife — brain is normal with a few nodes lit up.

"After": Man takes cocaine, all brain nodes lit up, he is running around yelling at kids, yelling at referee of kid's baseball game, crazy.
(Asterisk: not all people who scream at a referee at a kids' game are on drugs—they just act like they are.)

"After after": Brain looks like a war zone, all grey, demolished, nodes limp and out of commission, man sitting in car while kids play, head on steering wheel, then throwing up.

It's the same with any addiction.

Black cloud comes back bigger. Goes gambling again.

Black cloud comes back bigger. Goes running again.

Black cloud comes back bigger. Eats again.

Black cloud comes back bigger. Gets a fifth of whiskey.

Black cloud comes back bigger. Starts playing another video game.

The usual goods aren't enough to activate the pleasure centers.

Addiction in the Body

> *Guy on drugs, snorting cocaine, not interested in great meal. Gets thinner and thinner. Brain center for "meat", "fat", and "sweets" all pooped nodes, can't get up.*
>
> *Athlete taking heroin. Stops running. Weaker and weaker. Brain center for "feeling fit" all pooped nodes, can't get up.*

Only each time you take the drug, each time you do the habit, the pleasure nodes get more worn out. There are no more chemicals left to release. Each time the high is less, the crash bigger.

> *Repeating taking drugs, each time fewer nodes light up.*

So take more—heroin, or cocaine, or meth, or alcohol to get any pleasure.

> *Guy snorting some.*
> *Next time snorting a lot more.*
> *Next time more, and then more.*
>
> *Ditto alcohol.*
>
> *Ditto heroin injections.*

It's called TOLERANCE. Your body needs more to get the same or even *any* effect.

Taking drugs also starts to shrink the control center. Can't say NO.

> *Addict's brain. Control center getting smaller and smaller. Then just a very small area with a sign*
>   *"OUT OF BUSINESS".*

And after enough times, it's not good at all. But you really want it because with all those nodes busted and the wiring changed, you get terrible crashes when you don't take the drug. It's called WITHDRAWAL.

> *Nausea*   *Diarrhea*
> *Depression*   *Fever*
> *Sweating profusely*   *Hallucinations*
> *Vomiting*   *Rapid heartbeat*
> *Muscle aches*   *Crashing against walls*
> *Chills*

Alcohol is different—it makes you tired, it confuses you, and it shuts down the control center.

Man drinking alcohol—in the brain are waves of alcohol spilling over the control center, wiping it out till it dries out, but then still not as good.

Alcohol leaves you with all impulse—which feels like fun until you get beat up or fall asleep in the street. Alcohol blocks bad feelings—or creates them.

Man drinks alcohol, smiling, happy—then tells friends he's OK to drive. All impulse. Gets in fight and beat up. Crashes car. Asks rescuer to give him his bottle of whiskey.

Woman drinks, gets nasty, wants to fight. Then sad and tries to kill herself.

But stopping alcohol all at once can kill you!

Guy drinking a bottle of whiskey. Then next day a bottle and more. Then in jail, can't get alcohol, has seizures, and dies.

*   *   *   *   *

All addictions affect the control center, shrinking it—you're on just impulse.

We say that an addict craves the drug. But that's way wrong, for you can crave a chocolate bar and not get it, big deal. No, it's a lot worse than that.

Hot sun, desert, guy sweating, walking, discards shirt, discards hat, sweating more. Clearly in distress. Write "THIRST—must have water!" He struggles on along a path. There is a big bag of gold; he passes by. There is a beautiful woman he passes by. There is a big steak; he passes by. There is a baby crying, close to being attacked by a wildcat; he passes by. All because he can see a pitcher of water in the distance. He gets to the water. He drinks, then draws more water, drinks. Then satisfied. Then thinks about the gold, woman, steak, and baby, but they have all gone.

That's what addiction is like. You don't choose to have the drug. You can't live without it.

You know it's bad, you know it's hurting you, but you can't stop.

You dare not think about all the bad you're doing or the good you're passing up—that's too painful on top of need for the drug or gambling or alcohol. You're in DENIAL.

> *Girl drunk. Gets up, looks like hell, smokes, finds a beer, gives some to her child, drinks, belches.*
>
> *Doctor: You're getting cirrhosis of the liver. You've got to stop drinking.*
>
> *Girl: Sure, and I saw you at the bar last week. Anyway, I don't drink too much. I've cut down.*

Opioids are for pain—some people need them to function at all.

> *Veteran without legs, pain, can't function. Then takes opioid, able to get out of house, gets a job, able to work.*

But they also set up the same addiction. Some can stop.

> *Woman with back operation, pain, given opioid, then three weeks later stops taking them.*

But a lot of people can't stop once they've started. They're "primed for it", ready. Because of their brain wiring? Because of the way they were raised? Because everyone's doing it? Because they can't get any work to make them feel they can do something good? One week, even a few days, and they can't stop.

> *Man with severe cut on hand. Given opioids. Can't stop taking them many weeks later.*

If it's there, take it. More and more. They don't want to feel "normal" anymore.

The NEW NORMAL = deep in the drug or deep in the running or deep in the gambling.

> *Same girl in a bar. "I'll have just one", then another, then another until clearly out of it and taken out by a terrible looking man.*
>
> *A guy taking cocaine, snorts it. Great. Ten minutes later someone offers more, he takes it. Then again, at party. Child kissing his face, tugging at him passed out on floor.*

Woman gambling, husband takes her away from it, no money, back to kids. Later she rushes back to gamble more.
   "I'm just having a little fun."

*   *   *   *   *

REPAIR? Withdrawal. OUCH.

Someone going through withdrawal. "HORRIBLE"
Child trying to help but person can't feel the child.

HOW TO STOP???
Fear won't work. Any threat has less horrible consequences than not getting the drug or not gambling.

Person with thought bubbles: one of prison, one of drugs.
Goes off and gets the drugs.
   "It can't happen to me."

Girl told by a friend on the street that he's got HIV from the needles. She says, "Yeah" dopily, then shoots up.

And the control center is also part of foreseeing consequences—such as being in prison and not getting drugs for years. But the control center isn't working.

Addict's brain. Small control center. No imagination.
Compared with normal person's—thought bubble imagines in jail.

You can't FORCE someone to give up drugs.

Taking drugs. Caught selling them. Goes to jail.
Shows 4 weeks. 8 weeks. 4 months. No drugs.

Sure she'll look normal again, putting on weight, feeling better.

Before: skinny, acne, shaking, her hair is straggly,
   crazy look, fights.
After: plump, skin clear, hair good, calm.

But IT WASN'T HER CHOICE!

Resentful. Guards.
Lying in bed in the jail cell, looking up at ceiling, thought bubbles of bad she's done, of being abandoned, depressed, anxious. Thought bubble of taking drugs with friends and feeling good.

So when she gets out . . .

> *6 months. She gets out.*
> *Goes to friends, gets heroin.*
> *Thinks "I know how much I need—just like before".*

She uses the same amount she did before. Only now her body isn't used to it. She's lost tolerance to the drug. It's too much.

> *Takes the drug. Goes into coma. OVERDOSE.*

This time she's lucky.

> *Ambulance, two sprays in nose, labeled Naloxone.*
> *She revives.*

Or you get an overdose from a batch of drugs that are too strong.

> *Buying pills—opioids. Guy says they're really good. Arrow with label "fentanyl" pointing to pill. Takes the pill. OD.*
> *Addict friends try to help but too dazed to do anything. Dies.*

You can't get addicts to give up drugs through fear. The control center is not just to stop BAD but to lead to GOOD. Fear isn't enough. You need something that makes you feel good that isn't drugs and isn't addictive.

> *NOT   Give up drugs and take up gambling.*
>
> *NOT   Give up gambling and take up drugs.*
>
> *NOT   Give up drugs and start running but can't stop.*
>
> *NOT   Give up smoking and start eating.*

GOAL! Need a goal, a sight of GOOD. A life you want to live.

*   *   *   *   *

We've developed to be social, to be loving—family, friends, empathy, touching.

> *As in cartoons of early humans. Many together socializing around a fire. Walking arm in arm.*

Living together, helping each other out, people survived better.

> *Someone sick on a litter being carried.*
> *Helping someone who's leg is cut.*

Sheep with one that has broken leg and bleating and others ignore it.

Hunting together and sharing meat.

Sharing berries.

Ones who were social survived. All together.

Someone diving into a river to save a child. Man dies, child saved, his family lives because family of child takes care of them.

Ones with brains that want to help passed it on to their children.

Mama's brain center for being social, loving, and kind lighting up as she cuddles baby. Baby's does, too.

This is so important for survival that our brains light up not just when we are helping and being helped but when we see or hear about someone else helping another person.

Same scene saving child. Those who see it have the nodes in their social-loving-kindness center light up.

That's what got us to live with dogs, which helped us a lot. Empathy and caring from the dogs and to the dogs helped us become more social and to survive.

Hunting with dogs.
Dogs guarding, barking at lions.
Petting dogs, sleeping with a dog.

BEING LOVING. That's a goal, a sight of a good life we can all go towards. Empathy, social, touching, helping, being helped.

Addict after withdrawal. Imagines a life of caring and giving. Starts to live it, bit by bit. Pleasure nodes start to work again. Control center starts to grow.

Slow repair, as the control center begins to function a little.

Then finally eating a little. Ice cream. Tiny bit of pleasure. Control center with sign "UNDER REPAIR—Opening Soon".

Lighting up pleasure nodes when helping. Control center says "Back in Business—Directions to the GOOD available here".

It's not just feeling good by doing good. It's JOY that comes.

> *A smile from someone and person feels joy.*
>
> *A thanks, and someone feels joy.*
>
> *Helping someone who's hurt and not waiting around for thanks and just a big smile, JOY.*

Repair takes a long time! Habits replaced by new habits. HABIT is strong.

> *Smoker, trying to give up. After breakfast, going out the door, has to have cigarette.*
>
> *Heroin addict, goes to the street corner where he had friends, they are there and offer heroin again.*

It's not "Just say no". It's "Just say no" again and again and again and . . .

> *Car mechanic, "It's a big job come back in a week."*
>
> *Person helping addict, "It's a big job, we'll help and be helped for a long time."*

It takes a long time for cocaine and heroin addicts to get pleasure from what we do every day and to slide past depression. It takes a really long time for meth addicts and smoking addicts.

IT IS POSSIBLE.

> *Addicts slowly living better over time, pleasure in small things.*

Seeing a good life makes you feel GOOD. Kindness, being loving, generous, feeling the power of a loving heart. Can do it—with help. And that help is part of the GOOD: empathy, being social. We can't force it because fear and punishment don't help us learn new paths to a GOOD LIFE that make us feel GOOD.

> *With a family. Taking care of child. Helping others.*
>
> *Or no family, alone but loving heart, helping others.*
>
> *All together.*
>
> *A child says "I want to be like her."*
>
> *A child says "I want to be like him."*

Brain: lots of pleasure nodes light up a little, big smile on the control center.

Still . . .

The WANT is strong.

Minor version of the thirst cartoon.

DENIAL is strong.

Denial cartoon.

HABIT is strong.

Habit cartoon.

FEAR is strong.

Fear cartoon.

How do we get to wanting a good life?

How do we get to seeing a good goal?

Read about that in the next comic book
Helping Addicts—Helping Ourselves.

THERE IS NO WAY TO PEACE. PEACE IS THE WAY.

Poems

Dog Day's Song

Come, let me sniff your soul
    (dogs are not so different),
Whiff why poochie smells the hole
    (tales wag over our scent).

Sensing here essential odor
    probe we with our mind's wet nose.
        If your soul is pleasing to me
            and my scent's for you the same,
        We will frolic, bark our laughter,
            gambol out love's doggy game.
Dogs and we know joy is found here
    where there's little smell of rose.

The ferret, the spider, . . .

The ferret, the spider, the dog,
Yes even the soft brown puppy
She cancels, stuffs into the bag
As they leave my mouth
And turns, exasperated, afraid,
No more.
Be still.
I swallow hawks and doves and
Weasels and nuzzling goats,
She fears.
Her animals are all untended,
Whimpering, growling, hungry
They whine; she will not say them.
Nor I, save here.
Save her.
Say: her.

These days the spirit tries to rest

These days the spirit tries to rest.
Searching, searching; and as if fumbling to comprehend
    machinery, a clockwork too complex,
        wears, tires itself in the trying.
Even a peace that does know bounds is good;
    but outside, inching, trembling at the softness of those bounds
    for the entrance, the clear path, searching,
    searching, the spirit wears, tires itself.
The bounds are permeable; inside the darkness
    of rest, the golden warmness of peace, that
    the spirit, hard with trying, cannot pass.

I have called . . .

I have called for the love of the universe to flow into me, unconditional, all-embracing, everlasting. Called, lay peacefully and waited, relaxed and waiting. Called. Eliminating hope, and waiting. Lay still and sensed a slow tide, no flow but a sometimes trickle. Meditating on oneness that was not there.

And today I misspoke myself in my mind. Lost, a reverie slipped, and called for the love of the universe to blow into me. Blow! And I heard the rush of the winds from every heaven, air and heaven and the strong Bull in the sky, rush, blowing into my body. Blowing, until I burst—A body burst, and the stars, and the sky, and I neither I: only stars and the sky where once was I, black and light, the heavens had come to my call, bursting forth with power of the wind to blow apart the little case of flesh that was I.

California is not London

The fog comes in like a ghost of a horse
Halting and prancing from its home in the sea
With no direction but the memory of salt, lost
Among the dry brown hills
Now moist and fragrant, but
Cold.
The dream, too, lost in the gray
Memory of sunshine that will not last.
Tomorrow we will be happy.
There is no fire, no hearth
To plan and await the sun.
This is California and every fog is an
Interruption
Lost, swirling, running and remembering its
Home in the sea
And we, our homes on the land far from the sea
Turning, prancing, trying to remember the sunshine we have sought.

HOPE

Like a child running for a butterfly
We chase our fancy
Half crouched we spring for the sunlight
On a thin curved wing of hope we fly.

Cold, despondent, the twilight sits us
Rocked by a windless breeze.
Waiting for a gentle hand to touch us
We press our hope like clay.

Monday night at the observatory

The dome opens and the cold January air
Rushes in with the stars.
Through the telescope points of light still
Points of light, a nebula or galaxy
Painted on the dome of heaven.
If points of light are worlds and suns
Then words are trees and dogs,
And poems telescopes to see them better.
These points of light, these words—I trust them not,
But rest upon the darkened shapes that
    hover round the telescope

If we were all birds

If we were all birds,
    we'd all fly.
If we were rabbits,
    we'd multiply.
But we're not.

Five poems in the style of the Chinese

DOG BARK MIDDLE NIGHT
COCK VILLAGE DAWN
SLEEP ABSENT SLEEP ABSENT
WOOF CREE-CREE

LEAF WATER FLOAT
FISH GULP
OOPS

SUN HOT SHINE HOT SWEAT
TREE BRANCH SPIKE SHADE-NO
SHE VOICE WATER ROCK RIPPLE
DRINK DEEP

DOG BARK
CAT RUN
LIFE GOOD

YOUNG BEAUTIFUL
OLD UGLY
NO FIT

Stories and . . .

Jewish Dogs

I often studied late and did not like to be disturbed. But already at 10 o'clock I was restless. The winter had finally broken this week; instead of cozy my room seemed stuffy now. The damp smell of the new earth came up, and the branch that rustled against my window had small buds. I got up to shift away my unease, thinking that the peasants called this the rutting season. My attic room was small— I could nearly touch both walls when I stretched, and the slanted roof was occasionally a nuisance. I was about to return to the commentary on the Mishnah, half wanting to walk out in the Spring, when there was a knock.

This was a surprise. In the small town of Szczem everyone slept when it was dark, except for a few studious men and Gitle the insomniac. "One moment," I said, and tucked in my old shirt. I opened the door, about to say "Come in" when I stopped. I blinked— could this be, two dogs? What kind of joke is this? Maybe Moishele the Jester?

"I do hope we're not disturbing you," the one said. A dybbuk, I thought, or my overworked mind. I had been reading how Rabbi Eleazer ben Aruf had explained the line, "Even by how he treats his dog shall ye know your neighbor."

"We would have preferred to come during the day, but that was not possible. May we come in?"

If this was a dybbuk it was a very polite one. Bewildered, I hardly saw them, but now after several weeks I can describe them to you. He was a large, very thin collie, and she was a light-colored full grown poodle that reminded you of a puppy in the way she walked. They entered the room as any couple might.

I had only one chair at my desk. Should I offer it to them? Just as the thought struck me she said, "Do you mind if we sit here on your rug?"

"Please, please do," I said, and they both sat back on their haunches. I began to react to them quite as if they were any two visitors, they comported themselves so naturally.

"We have come to you as we have heard that you have a love for animals."

"It's true," I said, "but the ones I have known have never spoken."

"Perhaps they had nothing to say," the poodle said. And then continued before I could reply, "We have been travelling a very long time and . . . "

"Perhaps I could offer you some water, or a biscuit."

"No thank you," the collie replied, "we have eaten. You should know that we are not paupers."

"But we need someone to intercede with the rabbi for us. Neither of us was raised very religiously. Myself, I became a free-thinker, and she is a quiet agnostic. But still, we do not like this in-between world, just travelling together. We would like to get married, according to all the laws."

"Will you speak to Reb Shmuel for us?" Shlep the collie added. "It is said that he is a compassionate man."

"But they will think me out of my senses," I responded, "if I'm not truly mad. You are after all, excuse my saying it, dogs."

"There are Jews everywhere," she said. "Because we happened to have been born in Minsk where the winters are very cold and are a bit hairier than others, should the blessings of the Torah be denied us?"

"It would set our minds at rest." Shlep added. "And if the community acceded to our wedding, we would settle here. I have thought of beginning a school. I teach mathematics. And Jetta writes, for the Yiddish weekly in Lublin."

We discussed. I explained that it was forbidden to marry dogs. They said a Jew was a Jew. They were not eloquent, but reasonable. Could they be devils, tempting us to profane the synagogue and the Holy Scroll? But a devil would speak more brilliantly, not like two semi-educated free-thinking Jews who wanted to settle and make a living. Finally I agreed—what harm would it be? At most a curiosity, I reasoned. Already I was under their spell.

Isaac Bashevis Malamud

translated from the Yiddish
by Richard L. Epstein

Youth

Ahh. Youth. Age. Old age. We leave our dreams behind us. And at what price our dreams? My leg, shattered. My shoulders deformed from hobbling with a crutch so many years. Ahh. Youth. But I did it. I. This dream. Gone. That life is gone, that life is done, there is no life like that for me. I regret not one bit. Only . . . . Youth, and dreams, our hopes.

Come. Join me. Here by the fire. The stars are clear, no moon, just our fire, warm against the cold. I have a little sausage we can roast on the fire. It's a good sausage. But not the perfect sausage. A beer?

I grew up in Iowa. In Des Moines, a big town, but just a large farm town when I was growing up. In the countryside corn, and more corn to the horizon. Only a few trees along a stream or gully, then more corn. In June the light green, then deeper and deeper green as the tall stalks of corn grow high. Every summer I went to the farm of my Uncle Abe and Aunt Sadie. I learned to hoe their garden, to walk behind the tractor—but never on the tractor, Aunt Sadie said that was too dangerous. Seeing the tractor and all the big implements—so long ago I can't remember what they're called—cutting and then tossing the ears of corn into the wagon. Then home, shucking corn for dinner. The sweet, sweet corn. And pigs, not many, a few for sale and one or two for meat in the winter. Slaughtering a pig, with due reverence, never any alcohol or joking. Just Uncle Abe and a neighbor or two, and I, standing back, looking on. They would shoot the pig, in the head, quickly it died. Then they cut its throat, blood gushing to be caught for sausages. Then boiling water on the skin, scraping the bristles, and cutting open the carcass from neck to tail, the guts coming out. All saved for sausages. Steaming, the heart, the liver, all delicacies, some to be fried now for us as we worked, or really as they worked and I carried the meat in trays or bags to Aunt Sadie and the neighbor ladies, all laughing and talking, cutting the meat into smaller parts, washing the intestines—what a smell! A hug, a kiss, then back to the men and the real work.

Later we would fry the rind, chittlins we'd call the fried fat with just a little bit of skin and meat so hard you couldn't chew it, just the sweet juicy fat fried crispy. The men washed up and laughing, the women serving and joking, jokes I never understood about sausages and men, beer—even I got a sip.

The next day Aunt Sadie would begin to make the sausages for the winter. They were the sweet kind, just the meat—which she would grind in an old, old metal meat grinder she attached to the counter— and a little basil. Meat and the fat all ground up, pink, stuffed into a piece of intestine, tied up at either end. Ohh, those were good, those sausages. Fried for dinner, with tomatoes and lettuce from the garden in the summer, or with potatoes fried in the same fat in the winter. Sweet sausages. To eat them was heaven, dripping from my chin. Happy. Fat and chewy, and Aunt Sadie saying, "Eat, eat! Grow my little boy." And Uncle Abe smiling, saying, "Enjoy. Remember the good work we did to get this sausage. You helped. And remember the pig. She died, but nothing was wasted." All good. The sausage so sweet, the slight taste of corn in it, almost a memory of corn.

And then the other kind of sausage Aunt Sadie made. The ones she did as soon as she could with the blood collected at the slaughter. Blood mixed with the meat she was grinding. Stirred. Then stuffed into the big piece of intestine. No spices, just blood and meat. Dark sausages. And when we ate them later, cooked in a tray in the oven, they were black, yes really black, so dark, and a humid, earthy taste to them, a dark taste, so strong.

Ahh. The best days when I was very young. All caring and caring, eating and laughing, and work, hard work. We earned what we ate, and it tasted better for that.

I thought that one day I would make sausages, too. The sausages were good, but couldn't they be better? Made with spices, like we used at home, the oregano, the thyme, garlic we used when mother cooked hamburger or fish, the dill, the fennel. Not just salt, but pepper, too. We lived in the city, and I'd eat at my friends' homes, some Italian, some Polish, all different. There was no joy from eating what we'd worked hard to get, but the tastes were grand. Couldn't there be a better sausage?

I tried cooking. Mother laughed, it was so funny, her boy cooking. Was I going to be a mama's boy? That's women's work. But I loved to be in the kitchen, with the smells, the pots, the pans, spatulas and sharp knives, the jars of spices lined up on the counter, butter in the fridge, flour, sugar, salt, all ready. I learned. I made such a mess, my mother said. But she indulged me. Why not? And my father saw how much I loved to cook, he joked and said I'd be a great chef some day. Everyone would come to eat my dishes. But always I was thinking of sausages. Of a better sausage. Aunt Sadie would only laugh when I was with her as she made the sausages, suggesting this spice or that—she had so few in her kitchen I brought them with me. But she wouldn't let me make sausages my way. Never. There was the right way to make sausages, she knew, and that was what we would have. "Didn't you like my sausages last year, my little one?" I could only nod. She, Uncle Abe, they didn't understand.

So I experimented at home. What awful concoctions we tried. Even mother, smiling and generous, couldn't eat them, couldn't say a good word. I wanted to be a great maker of sausages, but I was hopeless. I was so young. And what tasted strong to me seemed almost bland to the older folks. Still, I could tell that though I hadn't made a really good sausage, and though the sausages that Aunt Sadie made were good, there was better to be made, better sausages. Perhaps, in the end, the perfect sausage.

I finished high school. I was a good student, not great, but good enough. My parents were so proud seeing me walk with cap and gown to get my diploma, handed to me by the principal, the band playing Pomp and Circumstance. My friends, too. We were happy. Betsy, not my girlfriend because we both were so shy, but my friend and perhaps one day . . . . We kissed that night, the first time. Oh heaven. Ahh. Youth. No kiss sweeter, never, in all the years that followed. No hair more yellow-white and soft, no skin more smooth, no eyes more laughing and caring than Betsy. My heart. But no regrets.

Betsy and my friends, well not all of them, went to college. Almost all to Iowa State University or the local junior college, or some to the University of Iowa farther away. A few even went to Minnesota, and one, Archie, went to Arkansas. My parents encouraged me. What would I do? They were so happy to see me graduate from high school, so proud. Did I want to do more? They would help, they had some savings. I could work in the summer—no, not at Uncle Abe and Aunt Sadie's because they had no money to pay me. Would I study more?

But no. I knew what I should do. I should go out into the world, see so much. Not wanderlust, but a great urge to meet others and taste their cooking. To find out the many tastes and smells, so one day I could make the perfect sausage. You laugh. I couldn't tell anyone. I tried to tell Betsy, who was going away to the University of Iowa in Iowa City in the fall. She smiled. I was so enthusiastic. So excited. I worked hard that summer, earning enough I was sure to travel a lot. O Youth! The few dollars seemed so much and was so little when I began my travels. Betsy loved that I had a dream. But it was a peculiar dream. She wanted to study literature and then, not so far away, have a family, some children. She was not a dreamer. No! That's not right. She was a dreamer, too. She dreamed of a home and family, a small house, cooking and laughing with her children as our parents had been with us, a good man, a provider. That was her dream. A common dream, but no less a dream and filled with hope. She couldn't really understand my dream. So peculiar. To find and make the perfect sausage? So odd. The enthusiasm was great, but the goal? She didn't encourage me, but she didn't discourage me. Too bewildered by my dream to encourage me.

The fall came. School began, my younger brother and sister off to their classes every morning, Betsy and my friends moved out to dormitories at college, some friends still with their folks going to the junior college. The leaves turning, brown, dusty brown already. My money from working at the grocery store in my pocket. It was time. My parents fearful. My father putting a little money in my hand, not much for he had not much, my mother making up sandwiches and, yes, some of Aunt Sadie's sausages in a bag, checking that my clothes were all in order in my knapsack. They couldn't understand. But they loved me. I'll never forget that. The love as they not only raised me but respected me, giving me their blessing as I went to seek my dream, letting me make my own mistakes. They couldn't even warn me of the mistakes I might make, for my dream, my journey was so far from any life they had lived. Perhaps I would find the perfect sausage. But if not, I was always welcome at home, there was always a place, whether I was 18 or 50, I could return and find again mother laughing in the kitchen, and my father talking with me after work. My father had no warnings, but took me away to the living room, to the big chair where he sat me down, the chair that he always sat in when he read the paper. He told me to always be kind, to be generous, never to let an opportunity to be generous pass by, for that would be the only regret I would have. To be kind. And respectful. And never to forget that I know

what is right and what is wrong. Then he stood me up, embraced me—
I can hardly remember when he had embraced me before—gave me a
kiss on my head and shook my hand. Mother came into the living
room. She said for me to be a good boy, to be helpful, and to remember
them, to remember all my family. I nodded. A little impatient. It was
time to go, to catch my bus. But though I was only half there, my
dreams already leading me on, I remember all they said, how they
looked, the love they gave me, that last time I ever saw them.

      If we knew the end, would we ever begin?
      Yes! Youth!

Arfito to Uschi

Arf!

Yesterday was good. When it was still dark Bidú started howling--there's this wailing sound in the distance, over by where Bidú likes to go to see his girlfriend. Then I started barking. I guess the big guy was excited, too, because I could hear him yell from that dark room on the corner. When it was light Bidú and I went for a walk. Chocolate came a little way, too. Chocolate likes to play with me, but I have to get him started. We nip at each other's ears and muzzles. He growls but his tail is wagging. Then the big guy started moving around in the house--we could hear him. We waited, and he came out later with that good meat in a can. He always gives Chocolate some first, then me, then he calls Bidú but Bidú is too lazy and won't get up so the big guy goes over to Bidú and gives him some of that meat. It is so tasty! Wow! I love it. Then he gives some to Chocolate and then some to me again. It is so hard to wait, and when he gives the meat to Chocolate, I try to get some too, but the big guy pushes me away. Then he went with Chocolate to the back yard—I know I'm supposed to sit outside the gate—and gave him some of that dry dog food. Not as good as meat, but plenty good. Why not me? I was excited. Then he went inside and came out and gave me a bone with a little meat on it and a bone with meat on it to Bidú. Heaven! Then it got hot, but the big guy did something with an oil on the rails to the steps. It was getting hot. Chocolate stayed in the shade next to the shed, and I stayed in the shade under the tree, and Bidú just stayed where he always stays under the big rose bush that's under the window where the big guy yells at us sometimes. When the big guy was hot, he went into the house, but he left the rag with the oil and I got to play with it. Fun. Before he went in, he came over to me and petted me, and then he went to Chocolate and petted him, but it was hot so we weren't too excited. Then we slept, Bidú, Chocolate, and me. Bidú always sleeps under the rose bush, and Chocolate in the big weeds where it's dark and cool, and I sleep in front under the tree where I can be close to the door where the big guy comes. Then later some truck comes up and parks in front of the house and I bark and the big guy

---

Arfito, who was just one year old, wrote this to Arf's dear friend Uschi on August 17, 2020 when Arf was going through chemotherapy and radiation treatment for prostate cancer.

comes out and a man in the truck gets out and they talk and the man goes back in the truck and leaves. And the big guy pets me and Chocolate. Later the big guy came out and we all three thought we were going for a walk—it's been a long time since we went for a walk. The big guy—that's stupid, I call him "Arf" because that's what he always says to us--, well Arf walked OK but just to the ditch and we all three went in, Bidú, me, and Chocolate, while Arf sat there. We love to go into the water on these hot days. Odd that Arf never goes into the water—he looks and smells hot. Then he gave us our dinner. First he gives Chocolate some of that dry food, then he takes some and gives it to me outside the fence and then some to Bidú. Did I tell you that sometimes he comes out and plays a little with us? He doesn't walk much now. I could hear him making something for him to eat, near to dark, and smell it too, hamburger! Wow. But we didn't get any. Later, when it was dark and I couldn't hear any of that strange voice that comes from the back where there's some funny light that I can see through the screen on the door, Arf came out. That's a really good time for Arf and me. He sits down on the top step and I sit next to him, real close. He puts his arm around me and rubs my belly and I lick his ear. He holds me real close and then sort of I lie down and he begins to rub my belly! How does he know that I like that so much??? It's wonderful. But not for too long. I get up. A couple nights ago he was almost all skin that I could lick and I licked his leg and then went behind him and licked along his back. It smelled funny and maybe I could help, like when I lick when I hurt. Then the lights went out and I prowled around a bit, Bidú got up to walk around, Chocolate went back to the weeds to sleep. And Bidú and I were ready to bark and be sure everything is safe here. I wonder what tomorrow will be?

Chocolate　　　　Arfito　　　　Bidú

The Devil's Dictionary—an update

civilized = us

uncivilized = them

torture = what they do to our prisoners; called "enhanced interrogation techniques" when we do it to their people

barbarians = people who speak and act and whose ways of killing we consider inferior to ours

savages = people who haven't learned to kill as well as we

bad guys = people who kill, torture, and destroy in order to further their political aims against us

good guys = people who kill, torture, and destroy in order to further their political aims for us

conservative Christian = someone who will kill for Christ

patriotism = the first refuge of scoundrels

social drinker = someone who drinks alcohol and hasn't yet been caught for DWI

pacifist = an evil person who contaminates our children's minds by telling them it's wrong to kill; a follower of Christ's message

Muslim = someone who follows the message of Mohammed

Muslim terrorist = common term now used in place of "Muslim"

liberal = someone who wants to use your taxes to pay for what he thinks will do others the most good

conservative = in politics, one who believes that we should conserve the political structure and laws as they are as much as possible, avoiding change (now archaic)

dog = a canine creature that brings love and warmth to a human family

cat = a feline carrier of toxoplasmosis; sacred to little old ladies

pervert = someone who does what we don't dare to do (or think), like putting mayonnaise on pastrami; see also "barbarian" *born-again Christian* = someone who by revelation has accepted the message of Christ to love one's neighbor as oneself and tries to compel his neighbor to feel the same

Gaza = a large concentration camp for Palestinians set up by Israelis on the model of the Warsaw Ghetto in WWII

God = the supreme ruler of all, omnipotent, omniscient, not perceptible to us through any of our senses, and unknown to many of us; corruption of "DOG", the deity of a suppressed religion

illegal military orders = military orders

conscientious objector = someone who believes that the commandment "Thou shalt not kill" does not have an asterisk next to it

good war = any war we participate in the day after one of our soldiers is killed

support for the troops = aid and succor to people who are paid to kill for us

strict constructionist = someone who believes the constitution should be construed literally as the words meant at the time it was written, except for the 2nd Amendment where "arms" is meant to include 50-caliber machine guns, not just muskets and sabers

stock broker = a gambler, with your money

realist = someone who has lost his or her ideals

naive = someone who is not a realist

Buddhist = a follower of the way of Buddha, except in those countries where Buddhists are in power

capitalist = someone who believes the best organizing principle for a society is greed

socialist = someone who believes the best organizing principle for a society is caring for your neighbor; now a pejorative

gay marriage = an institution designed to allow homosexuals to suffer in the same manner as heterosexuals

anti-American = someone who believes that the U.S.A. could be a better place—without killing

inflammatory speech = what you say that I disagree with

teacher = someone who suffers abuse from children, administrators, and parents in order to educate our young; a minor deity

romantic = someone who prefers good stories over experience

Shakespeare and dogs

(Commentary on an article and letters about Shakespeare
in *The New York Review of Books*, sometime in the 1980s)

In an earlier exchange in these letters it was strongly suggested that Shakespeare was prejudiced against dogs. It is well to remember that in his time, and ours, followers of DOG, the Almighty, Creator of All, were liable for death if uncovered. There are, nonetheless, clear signs in two of the most emotionally charged scenes in his plays and in one of his deepest sonnets that Shakespeare was a crypto-dogist.

In the earliest copies of his works, preserved through the centuries by followers of DOG, we find the following.

Hamlet says:
> For in that sleep of death, what dreams may come
> must give us paws.

Macbeth says:
> Tomorrow, and tomorrow, and tomorrow creeps in this
> petty pace to the last syllable of recorded time. And all
> our yesterdays have lighted fools the way to dusty death.
> Arf, arf brief candle . . .

And Sonnet 66 reads
> Tired with all these, for restful death I cry,
> As, to behold desert a beggar born,
> And needy nothing trimm'd in jollity,
> And purest faith unhappily forsworn,
> And gilded honour shamefully misplaced,
> And maiden virtue rudely strumpeted,
> And right perfection wrongfully disgraced,
> And strength by limping sway disabled,
> And art made tongue-tied by authority,
> And folly, doctor-like, controlling skill,
> And simple truth miscall'd simplicity,
> And captive good attending captain ill.

> Tired with all these, from these would I be gone,
> Save that, to die, I leave my dog alone.

It is well to remember that in Shakespeare's time as now "Lady" was a common name for a dog. The Sonnets fall into place and gain clarity when we understand that the Dark Lady was a black German shepherd, and the young, fair boy was a collie. What other than our prejudices prevents us from considering that the obscurity and confusion about sex in the Sonnets may come from a concern about an acceptable form of writing among the followers of DOG?

Plays

The Hanging Tree

Characters
>Old Man
>Young Man
>Young Woman
>Little Old Lady
>Poet

Scene

A 4 inch x 4 inch board is stretched across the stage from left to right, about 7 to 8 feet off the ground, through center stage. On it are tacked branches and leaves. There is a bench, about $1^1/_2$ or 2 feet high, running parallel with the "tree" and also almost from off stage to off stage.

* * * * *

A middle-aged man walks on.
He is carrying a noose, paper, and pen.

Old Man: A terrible weight is lifted off my shoulders now. That she should leave me, after so many years. But I don't begrudge her. I love her too much; and besides, what other choice had she? Linda, to whom nothing was ever too good, how could I still provide for you? A sagging business, a sagging old man. He deserves you Linda, whoever he is. I don't hate you, you simply had no choice. Just thank God I don't know him because the visions, darling Linda, sweet Linda.

No sense prolonging this unsufferable grief. Is all in order here? (looks at paper) Yes. You see here, Linda, I still love you. Everything I've left to you. Only to Jack I should leave something, too. Maybe the card table where we used to play? No, that'd be too morbid. Something he'll want to keep. A fond memento of me. Ah, my putter. He's always been envious of it. Fine, "To Jack Waters, my putter which can be found in my golf bag in the trunk of my car."

Well, goodbye, I guess.

He goes to the bench, gets up on it, puts his noose on the tree, gets ready, puts his head through the noose.

Just that I shouldn't struggle too much. I hope that it looks at least a little elegant.

He is ready to jump.
Enter a young man, also with noose. He is oblivious of Old Man. Goes to bench, climbs up on it, begins to put his noose on tree.

Old Man: Who are you? (*takes his head out of noose*)

Young Man: Don't do that, you nearly scared me to death.

Old Man: What're you doing here? Can't . . .

Young Man: Clearly I'm not here for a picnic. Can you see this? This is a noose. A noose. I'm going to hang myself. Ah, you wouldn't understand. Fat middle class establishment. You never did . . .

Old Man: Just a second young man. I may be sagging, a bit overweight perhaps, but I have never in my life been called fat before.

Young Man: See. You're all alike. You won't give a guy a chance, hear him out to the end. You all think that cause you're rich, you got money, that you rule the world, that you don't have to listen to anyone. It's guys like you that have created this lousy rat race here, this treadmill I can't even see the end of. Well, I'm getting out. I've had enough.

Old Man: Enough, enough of what? At your age what could you have had enough of? Why when I was, excuse me, but how old are you, 18?

Young Man: 20. 18, huh, I'll have you know that I've been getting away with buying beer for almost a year already.

Old Man: Beer. When I was 20 no one could buy beer. It was prohibition. We had our whole life ahead of us, there weren't too many choices then, it was the depression, but it seemed like the whole world to us.

Young Man: I've heard that before. Well, times have changed a lot since then. What've I got left to look forward to? Tell me that, huh? A college education.

Old Man: A college education. In those days I couldn't even have hoped for one.

Young Man: Well, in these days, I can hardly even hope for not one. I mean, if I cop out, what's left? Someday I'll be regretting it, doing some lousy job that God knows I'm too good for. So I got to get through it, through the exams, and the boring classes, and the coeds that wave their tails at you. And worse, I got to do well at it, I can't just get through, I have to get A's.

Old Man: But if you hate it, why? Why do you have to get A's?

Young Man: Because I want to go to graduate school. Anyway, what am I telling my life story to you for. What are you doing here?

Old Man: Well, until you interrupted, I was in the process of putting my head through this noose, and then, with a hint of delicacy, ending it all.

Young Man: Unh unh. Not here. I don't know about you, but I've been planning this out for a long time, and I didn't have any second corpse swinging from the same tree. I mean, how's it going to look when they come to find me with a second body there? What impact will it have? Answer me that.

Old Man: Not much, I have to admit.

Young Man: No, damn near none at all. Even with my note, they'll probably get it into their heads that it was a double suicide. How would that look?

Old Man: What would my friends think?

Young Man: That anyone would think that I'd have anything to do with you, much less . . .

Old Man: Well, you needn't get hostile. That's the trouble with your generation. No sense of moderation, no rationality, no ability to discuss. You just want to rave and expect all the troubles of the world to disappear. My generation worked.

Young Man: Well, if you did such a good job, why are you here now, with your "delicate" noose.

Old Man: Good point.

Young Man: Well, maybe you aren't so bad after all.

> *Enter a young woman. She is oblivious to the other two. She is also carrying a noose; she crosses the stage, gets up on bench, puts her noose on tree, sighs, breaks down, and starts crying.*

Old Man: Look at that will you.

Young Man: The nerve.

Old Man: We'll just have to tell her.

Young Man: Yes.

Old Man: Excuse me, but I'm afraid this tree is reserved.

Young Woman: Oh my god! (*scared, then continues to cry*)

Young Man: Yes, we were just discussing which of us had the right to this tree, and although there are a lot of branches to it . . .

Young Woman: How could you? How could you be so callous?

Old Man: I think our discussion was very well ended. I don't see how you planning ahead should have any bearing on it at all. I was here first.

Young Man: First come, first served, huh? Always the same with you establishment people, since you always have the money, you're always first.

Young Woman: If it's a matter of money, I haven't any. I always thought that at least this would be free.

Old Man: I'm afraid that this young blusterer has been exaggerating.

Young Man: Exaggerating?

Old Man: Yes, a common fault of youth.

Young Woman: Oh, how so?

Old Man: Well, you see I was here first. I was all ready to, well, you know.

Young Man: What's wrong, you can't say it?

Old Man: I was just thinking of her feelings. Besides, it is a bit coarse.

Young Man: He was going to "end it all".

Young Woman: Ah.

Old Man: When he came by, and tried to butt in.

Young Man: Me, butt in? Who scared who half out of his wits? Huh?

Old Man: I'm certainly sorry about that, but it wasn't my intention, I can assure you.

Young Man: Well, it doesn't matter. I'd been planning this for over a week, and he wasn't in my plans. Besides, I'm plenty old to decide what tree I'll jump from.

Young Woman: Jump. Jump you say? Oh, don't do that.

Young Man: No? Why shouldn't I?

Young Woman: It's so messy. I thought of it, too, but then I thought what if I don't die, but just break a leg, or land on my face and have to go through all that awful plastic surgery, and you never look decent afterwards. None of my friends would feel sorry for someone who's a really helpless cripple or who's repulsively disfigured. No, don't jump. A rope is much better.

Young Man: That's what I meant. It was just a figure of speech.

Young Woman: Oh.

Young Man: Anyway, why are you here?

Young Woman: I'm not sure I really ought to tell. Especially if I'm not even allowed to use this tree. Anyway, what's to stop me from coming back after you're done and doing it?

Old Man: Three bodies? Now, that's not so bad. Especially with a young girl. She wouldn't feel sorry for me, but she'd remember all right. And maybe Jack would get a thrill out of it.

Young Man: See. Approaching senility. He's talking to himself.

Old Man: Well, I don't see any reason that we can't just all use this tree. I mean we're all rational people. We can surely work our differences out. It's just a matter of time.

Young Man: Ah, for a girl it's O.K. But for me, no. What kind of male chauvinist pig are you?

Old Man: I beg your pardon. A male . . . a male what?

Young Man: Chauvinist pig. You know, you put women down.

Old Man: Me, me put women down? Look, it's O.K. if we all, *all* of us use this tree, see. But you've got to know that I don't put women down. Ha, that's a laugh. You don't see me walking out on my wife of 16 years. No, I've more respect for a woman than that. No, you try to be a decent guy, and everyone walks all over you.

Young Man: Hey, I'm sorry. You know, it's just a term. We're all trying to liberate ourselves from roles. It's not easy for any of us. You know, we just don't give women a chance, let them have jobs, treat them like people.

Old Man: Well, I'll bet that's not why you're here.

Young Woman: No.

Old Man: See.

Young Woman: I, I just feel lost. I was always very shy, and my shrink, psychiatrist that is, well, he said I should open up more. I've been trying, really trying, but it's no use. People just don't like me.

Old Man: (*authoritatively*) Nonsense.

Young Woman: And they're always intimidating me and trying to tell me what to do, and how I feel, and how I don't feel. I just don't feel that I'm good for anything. It must be my parents.

Young Man: Yeah. I know. Mine too.

Old Man: Excuse me, but I don't understand. Your parents?

Young Man: Yeah, they screw you up when you're young and you don't have a chance. Like mine for instance. Always achieve, achieve. Hell, my mother even put up the list of the Presidents in the bathroom so that I should memorize them there.

Old Man: Well, it hardly seems fair to put all the blame on them. I mean, you have to accept some of the responsibility yourself. They're just people after all. They were probably doing the best job they knew how.

Young Man: Damn poor job, from my point of view.

Young Woman: Unfortunately from mine, too. But mine wasn't so awfully interesting.

Old Man: No?

Young Woman: I was just toilet trained too early. At least that's what my doctor said.

Old Man: Seems unlikely.

Young Man: Not at all, but then they didn't study psychology in the schools in your day, did they.

Old Man: You don't have to rub it in. I didn't go to college, you know.

Young Man: Oh, I'm sorry. I forgot.

Young Woman: It doesn't seem so bad to me.

Young Man: Which, going to college, or not going to college.

Young Woman: Not going. Why my doctor said it would be quite all right not to go to school if I didn't want to, but I didn't know where else to go. Besides, he has a degree on his wall, so he must have gone. To several in fact. Apparently it doesn't help you.

Old Man: It doesn't huh? Look at him, he's probably pretty well off.

Young Woman: Yes, but he's also pretty screwy. Oh don't get me wrong, I like him a lot, and he's a very nice person, . . .

Old Man: Yes?

Young Woman: But he always wants to talk about, well, . . . my sex life.

Young Man: The dirty old man. He'd probably like to . . .

Old Man: Hey, just cause someone gets old doesn't mean he's a pervert or something. Though it does sound like this guy might be.

Young Woman: Oh, he's quite delicate about it. Very nice really. He says that I don't have to talk about it if I don't want to, just to let it come out when I feel like it. But I just feel like he's sitting there with his little, pencil, hanging down, waiting for me to start talking dirty.

Young Man: You have had a hard time of it. Look, sex isn't dirty. It's a beautiful thing. I mean, think of it as an extension, how like when you love someone, it's the only way you can express yourself. It's beautiful.

Young Woman: Really? I never thought of it that way before.

Young Man: Trust me, I know it's beautiful. Like joy in the morning, the very thrill and ecstasy of a spring morning . . .

Young Woman: Oh, you mean that you've, that you've . . .

Young Man: No, but I've read a lot. I'm a very good student.

Young Woman: What's he doing?

>*Old man has gone back to his noose which is hanging there, and, leaning on it is crying softly.*

Young Man: Hey, what's wrong.

Old Man: You wouldn't understand, you're too young.

Young Man: That's a rather crass thing to say.

Old Man: I know. I'm sorry. It's just that you're right. It is beautiful. I know. She really is.

Young Man: Hey, don't start in on her again.

Old Man: Oh, no, not you, my wife. You see, she left me. Though I don't blame her.

Young Woman: Oh.

Old Man: Though I don't mean that you're not very lovely, it's just, well, it's just not the same.

Young Man: I can understand that.

Young Woman: You can?

Young Man: Sure.

Old Man: Well, let's get on with it.

Young Man: Except I'm afraid that's my rope.

Old Man: I'm quite certain that it's mine. See how delicately and skillfully I've done the knot?

Young Man: Well, when you're planning something for a week, you don't just throw it together. My knot was done, well, lovingly.

Old Man: Why don't we let you decide for us. Which knot do you think is better? Then that one will be mine.

Young Man: Yours?

Old Man: Of course, isn't that what we decided?

Young Woman: They both look alike to me. But then I'm not very good with knots. They are both done very nicely. Mine's a mess compared to these.

Young Man: Really?

Young Woman: Yes, see?

Old Man: It really wouldn't hold up at all. Here, give it to me. I'll fix it up.

Young Man: Butt out. Can't you see that she wants me to do it?

Old Man: You really do want him to, don't you. Well, I guess when you're old . . .

Young Man: That's right.

Young Woman: Oh, you needn't take it hard, it's just that, well you see . . .

Young Man: There, it's all fixed (he's put it back on the tree, yanks on it), doesn't seem like it'll give now.

Young Woman: Oh, thank you. I never was very good at mechanical things.

They all take their positions, with their nooses.

Young Man: Do you, do you mind if I hold your hand? I know it's really sudden and all, but I'd feel lots better about it.

Young Woman: Oh, please do.

Old Man: Kids. Don't hardly know their own mind.

Older lady comes on. She is oblivious to the others.
She is carrying a noose and a picnic basket.

Little Old Lady: Oy. My Danny. How could you? My Danny, my lovely Danny. From a boy I raised you. You used to sit on my knee, with your sweet angelic smile. And rosy cheeks. For you, Danny, for you I'm doing this. It should bring you back to your senses, to see what you've done to your poor old mother. Crazy you've driven me. You should always remember me. And for the funeral you shouldn't get hungry, I made a few things. I know you'd miss them if I just left them at home, so here, I'm putting them here, you shouldn't miss them.

She puts picnic basket on floor in front of bench, gets up on bench, fixes her noose to the tree, sees others, nods to them, looks like she's going to say something, decides no, puts her head through noose.

Old Man: Shouldn't have done WHAT?

Little Old Lady: I beg your pardon. It's to me you are talking?

Old Man: Yes, yes, what shouldn't he have done? You weren't going to go off like that and not let us know.

Little Old Lady: Oh, I didn't know you were listening. My name is Molly. And yours?

Old Man: Bill, Bill Jefferson.

Little Old Lady: And these two, they're yours?

Young Man: Heavens no. I never saw him before today. He's sure not mine.

Young Woman: Me either. Though you are a nice man.

Little Old Lady: Well, yes you do look very nice. Very smart, but you don't look like you've been eating well, not at all.

Old Man: You're right. My wife was a lousy cook.

Little Old Lady: Was? You mean she died? How sad. So young.

Old Man: No. She left me.

Little Old Lady: It's probably all for the better. If she's so dumb to throw away a nice man like you, she doesn't deserve you.

Old Man: Oh, I don't blame her. I'm getting old and . . .

Little Old Lady: Nonsense. Getting old. Look at me. Guess how old I am, just guess.

Young Man: A hundred.

Little Old Lady: Don't be smart alecky. Guess.

Young Woman: I think you're 73.

Little Old Lady: Well, it doesn't matter. Me, I'm 65 and I feel fit, except some times pains in my side I can't breathe sometimes when I think of Danny. And do I look it? No. I'll live a good ten, twenty years. Just see. Old? You've got the best years of your life ahead of you.

Old Man: I wish I could believe that.

Young Woman: I don't think I'll ever live to be *that* old.

Young Man: Me either.

Little Old Lady: And worries, worries, what worries do you have? Huh? Compared to me nothing.

Old Man: No, you don't think so? Well, . . .

Young Man: His are bad, but believe me . . .

Young Woman: You wouldn't want to hear my . . .

Little Old Lady: No? Listen. My son, Danny, my youngest boy.

All: Yes?

Little Old Lady: Two weeks ago he comes home, and he's got a beard. Oy.

Young Man: Is that all?

Old Man: If only he doesn't think the way they do, but just has it because he likes it. Maybe he isn't rebelling.

Young Woman: I kind of like beards.

Young Man: You do?

Young Woman: Yes. Although I never knew anyone who had one. As long as it wouldn't be scratchy.

Young Man: I had one once, but it got too itchy. I shaved it off. I was a lot younger then.

Little Old Lady: A beard. My Danny. Your sweet, angelic face. He has such rosy cheeks. Why should he cover them up? Answer me that.

Old Man: That's all? He grew a beard, so you're going to throw it all away at this tree?

Little Old Lady: Oh, also he got married with the girl he was living with and didn't invite me. But that, that I'm willing to forgive. The beard, no. No, that's a slap in the face to his mother.

Young Woman: Maybe if you told him.

Little Old Lady: Told him? Oy, so many times. He just doesn't listen. It's as if he were deaf. A mind of his own he's got. Never does he care about anyone else. I've got to do something to wake him up to his responsibilities. He can't be a child all his life.

Young Man: No? Why not?

Old Man: Even if he wanted to, he couldn't. We grow old.

Young Woman: "we grow old, we shall wear the bottoms of our trousers rolled." That was from T. S. Eliot, wasn't it?

Young Man: "I", "I grow old."

Young Woman: Oh.

Little Old Lady: Here I come for God knows what, and I meet such nice people. What are you doing here?

Old Man: Well, you see, since my wife left me, I didn't feel there was anything left for me. So, well, the end one is mine.

Young Man: Are you sure?

Old Man: Yes, remember. That way it worked out that you two could be together.

Young Man: Oh, yes, that's right.

Little Old Lady: And you came to watch?

Young Man: No. I never did like watching. Even when I was young I always wanted to be doing. I was going to jump too.

Young Woman: He doesn't really mean jump. It's just his way of saying, well, ...

Little Old Lady: Oh, I understand. Well, I hope I'm not interrupting anything. Go on, just pretend I'm not here.

Old Man: That just wouldn't be possible. But I guess we've decided that there's plenty of room here for everyone. ... You can just fix yours there, there on the end.

Young Man: On our side?

Old Man: Yes. I'm at the end of the branch on this side.

Young Man: Is it O.K. with you?

Young Woman: Sure.

Young Man: O.K. You can fix it up there where you were going to, but none of this watching. Either you're here for a reason or you go.

Little Old Lady: O.K., O.K., don't get upset. I'm old enough to be your mother.

> *They all take positions in nooses.*
> *Enter a young man, very soft featured.*
> *He too carries a noose.*

Poet: (*reading from a piece of paper*)

In all the days of yesterday,
And all the days tomorrow,
Will there ere be time enough
For laughter and for sorrow?

When the cuckoo cries of memories still
And the hopes of the summertimes' morrow,
Will the green fields wisp in the ripening sun
Will the ear stay tuned to the sparrow?

In the dreams of the autumn time's rockings,
In the hymns and the hills of the roe,
Does the eye still yearn to the gladed spot
Where the hunter steals by the doe?

Can smothered joys line our dreams tonight,
While sadness lies in the firelight?

Young Man: Oh, Jesus, that was awful.

Young Woman: It was pretty bad.

Young Man: I sure hope you plan to use that thing. *pointing to noose*

Old Man: Here, let me give you a hand. I've been here the longest, so I figure it's up to me.

> *Goes to take noose from his hand, sets up noose,*
> *Young Man guides him to a spot on the end.*

Little Old Lady: Wait, I didn't think it was so bad. I liked it. It brought back a lot of memories. From my youth. Could you say that part over again? About the deer?

Poet: Hey, hey wait a minute. Who are you?

Old Man: We're here to do what you're going to do, from the look of it.

Young Man: But you've sure got a better reason for it than I ever could.

Poet: Huh?

Young Man: If no one ever told you before, your poetry isn't very good. And especially when it's out of place when you interrupt four people.

Young Woman: I've read a lot of poetry, but I never read any like that.

Poet: Gee, I'm sorry, but I sure didn't think I was going to have an audience. I came here to be alone. To be with my thoughts for a few minutes. Before.

Young Man: Well, you sure left them strewn about.

Young Woman: I think he means your thoughts.

Old Man: When I was younger, I wrote a little poetry, too. But I stopped kidding myself.

Poet: You really didn't like it?

Little Old Lady: Oh I liked it very much. It reminds me of when I was a young. Like you.

Poet: I'm glad. I didn't really write it for anyone. At least not for anyone here. I was going to leave it with my note.

Young Man: Don't. Tear it up. People will remember you better.

Poet: Oh, I don't think so. Not Elizabeth anyway. By now she's probably not even thinking about me.

Old Man: Rejected?

Poet: Sort of. I've fallen in love, and she hardly knows I even exist. She's very beautiful. Long hair, radiant brown eyes. I, I become tongue tied whenever I'm with her. I just can't stand it anymore.

Young Woman: What has she said? Doesn't she like you?

Poet: Oh, she likes me. But she likes everyone. I'm not special. I'm just another guy to her.

Young Man: Women can be hard sometimes. You've got to hope. Eventually someone will come along *(looks meaningfully at Young Woman)*.

Poet: But when? When? I tried to read her some poems, I tried to make her understand. But she only wants to play tennis. She's the third one in less than two months. I can't stand disappointments like this. When she reads this poem, she'll understand.

Young Man: When I heard the poem I already knew.

Poet: Yes?

Young Man: That you had to kill yourself. Why don't you give up poetry and do something useful?

Poet: Like what?

Young Man: Good question. *(to Old Man)* Where were we?

Young Woman: Yes, you could make knots, nooses you know. Let's see how you did.

Old Man: Oh, I've already straightened it out. It wasn't too good to begin with.

Poet: No, I'm not very good at those things.

Young Woman: That's funny, neither am I.

Little Old Lady: Children. Aren't they lovely.

Old Man: Yes.

Poet: What's your name? My name's Robert.

Young Woman: Mine's Ellen.

Young Man: And mine's Don. And we were doing fine before you came. Now, if you don't mind, you've got the end there. Yes. On that side of this lady. And we're here.

Young Woman: You don't have to be nasty. And I can speak for myself you know.

Young Man: When did that start?

Young Woman: Soon enough. Excuse me.

Little Old Lady: Yes?

Young Woman: Would you mind awfully if we traded places?

Little Old Lady: No, of course not, but you'll have to help me move my things.

Poet: Gee, you're being really nice. Did you ever love someone?

Young Woman: No. I'm not sure I could love someone.

Young Man: Don't bother. I know she can't. At least this way I won't end up with a wife walking out on me after I get settled. Oh, Jesus, I'm sorry. I didn't even think what I was saying. I could just kill myself.

Old Man: Please go ahead.

Little Old Lady: I guess everything's in place. You're really a darling little girl. If only my Danny had met you.

> *They are all in position now.*
> *The Poet and Young Woman are holding hands.*

Old Man: Well.

Young Man: Well.

Poet and Young Woman: Well.

Little Old Lady: I only hope that the chicken soup and turkey shouldn't spoil before my Danny comes. I left a note for him.

Old Man: Excuse me, turkey?

Little Old Lady: Yes. You'd like a piece?

Old Man: Well, I am hungry. And it seems silly not to indulge myself this one last time. Would it be all right?

Little Old Lady: Certainly. (*to Young Man*) And you, you'd like some too? You're so thin, come, come eat, it'll do you good. Look, this can wait. Is the tree going anywhere?

Young Man: Well, it'd certainly be better than the cafeteria food they serve at the college. I guess it would be O.K.

Little Old Lady: And you two? You look silly, eat. You should share food; it'll bring you closer.

> *They are all down in front of the bench now, where a picnic cloth is spread, and a picnic banquet laid.*

Old Man: Very good.

Young Man: I haven't had a salad like this since I left home.

Little Old Lady: So why did you leave home?

Young Man: Some things are more important than food.

Young Woman: This sure is good. But with all my problems, if I get fat too, my psychiatrist will kill me.

Poet: I once wrote a poem about food. You really have to get into the image to appreciate it. I didn't eat for over a day so that I could concentrate.

Little Old Lady: Better you should eat.

Poet: I know that now. When you get older you get more mature. I look at the world a lot differently than I did just two or three years ago.

Old Man: I feel lots better. I guess I must have been hungry all right. I almost feel like it's given me a second chance.

Young Man: A second chance?

Old Man: Yes. After all, as you said, she'd have had to have been really dumb to leave me. And maybe the business is pretty low, but at least I've got a business, which is a lot more than most people.

Little Old Lady: Certainly.

Young Man: If I could eat like this every day maybe I wouldn't always feel so lousy. You eat at that cafeteria every single day and pretty soon you're not even hungry. It's depressing.

Little Old Lady: Well, you can always come to my home. There's always a place for a nice young man like you. You're very polite. You must have a very nice mother. I'm sure she cares for you a lot.

Young Man: Too much. But that's a really nice invitation. If you really mean it, could I come? I'd help around your house for you.

Poet: All I really wanted was just one more chance.

Young Woman: For me just *a* chance is enough.

Poet: (*to Young Woman*) That's all we can ever really hope for. That's why we keep on living. To have another chance. We always feel that it's in our hands, that if we believe then we can create another chance.

Young Woman: Oh, yes. And now I believe that, maybe, I can.

Little Old Lady: See, you eat right, you feel good all over.

Old Man: *I* certainly feel better.

Young Man: Me too.

Old Man: Look at that tree will you. Sturdy old fellow. Rough and strong. You're almost like a friend you know (*to tree*).

Young Man: I sort of feel the same way about it.

Poet: Oh tree divine, oh leafy vine . . .

Young Man: Cool it.

Little Old Lady: I think maybe we'd be more comfortable at my place. Nice chairs, a T.V. set. We could all enjoy.

Old Man: Here, let me help you (*they start to clean up*).

Young Man: Hey, can you give me a hand taking these down (*referring to the nooses*).

Poet: All right.

Little Old Lady: Is it all tidy?

Young Woman: Yes.

Old Man: Let's go.

They all leave the stage looking now as at the beginning.

*   *   *   *

The tree sheds its leaves to denote time passing. Enter the poet, carrying a notebook.

Poet: To Autumn:

There is a chill in the air, that wasn't there,
   before, before,
A crisp dry leaf, a pink cloud reef, the wind
   bore, it bore,
The brisk chill rustle, autumn's bustle,
   rising, rising
With a pale street light, winter's night,
   comprising,
A lonely eve, a time to leave,
   aspiring,
Homeward bound, from winter's ground,
   retiring.

No hope. No hope. If my dreams cannot come true I'm left no hope. First Ellen, then Marcia.

These poems are a sorry substitute.

But they're really all I've got. I just wanted to say goodbye tree, grass. You've been good to me, it's not your fault.

(*breaking down a bit*)

There is a chill in the air, that wasn't there . . .

Enter Young Man with a noose also.

Young Man: Oh, no, you again. Why don't you get on with it? You'll never get anything done standing there letting drivel come out of your mouth. I better be going.

Poet: No, stay, it's all right. She didn't want me either. It's a shallow pool to build your hope on, women.

Young Man: Yeah. Well, she was definitely screwy anyway.

Poet: I hope I didn't take your old place. If you were planning ahead or something, I wouldn't want to interfere in your plans.

Young Man: No. I've gotten older. Any place here will do. Besides, I like this old tree so much that any place is fine.

   He affixes his noose.

Poet: Why, why . . .

Young Man: Why am I back? I sure don't have to ask that about you, do I?

Poet: No, I guess not. It's pretty obvious.

Young Man: It's the pressure. Damned grades, damned work, and no peace, the noise, the cars, the radio. And my conscience. Who said I was supposed to solve all the world's problems, huh? Huh? Why me? Grades were bad enough.

Poet: If you're such a bad student, why don't you quit?

Young Man: Who said I was a bad student? That's the trouble, you start getting A's and you can't stop.

Poet: Oh, I never had that problem.

Young Man: No, I suppose not. This'll sure be a relief. I'll finally get it off my chest.

Poet: You don't mean (*points to his head*).

Young Man: Ugh no. I wasn't being literal. I mean the worries, the fatigue, the constant desire to scream.

Poet: Well, why didn't you scream?

Young Man: I did. They made me find another rooming house. Fourth one in less than a year. I can't stand the thought of moving again.

Poet: Well, I'm glad you're not angry with me anymore. I mean, after last time. It's best to go with friends.

Young Man: You? It was her. I should know by now. Women are all the same.

Poet: All?

Young Man: Yes, all the same.

Poet: Then there really isn't any hope.

> *Puts head through noose.*

Do you think it looks O.K.? You don't think the papers will blow away.

Young Man: No, it looks O.K. to me.

Poet: Shall, shall we . . .

Young Man: Yes.

> *Both have heads through nooses.*
> *Enter Young Woman. She is carrying a noose, sniffing more than slightly. Looking a bit stealthy. She begins to put her noose at the far end away from the others. She is oblivious to them.*

Poet: Look.

Young Man: Her. A fine time to come crawling back.

Poet: Ellen. Why, why . . .

Young Woman: Oh, God. (*she breaks down*)

Poet: What happened? Did, did . . .

Young Man: Hey, leave her alone. Remember. All the same. She doesn't want you, just a shoulder.

Young Woman: That's very unkind. You know Robert, that I like you. It's, it's just that you demand so much.

Poet: No more than I demand of myself.

Young Man: And that's damned little from the sound of your poems. Look, if you're back and you want to use this tree, go ahead. I'm not making any claims this time. We were all settled when you came, and no tears are going to screw up the scene this time, understand?

Young Woman: Uh huh. Will, will this end be all right? I don't take very much room.

Young Man: Anywhere's fine, let's just not talk about it.

Poet: Yes, let's get on. I wrote another poem. To Autumn. But you probably wouldn't understand anyway Ellen.

Young Woman: Oh Robert, how can you say that? Even if I don't love you, at least the way you want me to, I can still see the beauty in your mind.

Poet: You can?

Young Man: You can?

Poet: Listen. I call it Autumn, or Farewell to Tomorrow.

Young Man: God damnit, you got him started. They're all the same, remember? Come on, get up there.

> *He pulls him back to his place.*

A woman comes in and it's all ruined.

Young Woman: Some other time, Robert.

Poet: I'll always remember you Ellen.

Young Man: Jesus. Are we ready?

Poet: Yes.

Young Woman: Yes.

Young Man: On the count of three. One, two, . . .

> *Enter Little Old Lady, with another basket.*

Little Old Lady: Buckle my shoe, three, four, close the door.
Oy, how it takes me back, to when I held Danny on my knee.

Young Man: Damn.

Young Woman: You? It didn't work out then?

Little Old Lady: No. A mother can debase herself only so much. Then it's up to the son. No further, I said, no further. It's like his mother never existed. You'll see Danny, you'll see how I loved you.

Poet: You couldn't get along with his wife?

Little Old Lady: Which one? He got divorced. To that, too, he didn't invite me. He knows how all the time I watch Perry Mason, how I like what they do in courts, and does he invite me? No.

Young Woman: Which one? You mean he got married again.

Little Old Lady: If you could call it that. This time it's to a man. He writes he's very happy. But I wouldn't want to go visit. It's very sad when two young, nice boys can't find a girl for themselves. You know?

Young Man: We know.

Poet: But not that way.

Young Man: Thanks no.

Little Old Lady: I see you're all ready, already.

> *She takes noose out of basket.*

I'm always late, I'm interrupting, I'm sorry. Fast I'll fix this here, please young man, can you help me? I'm too old to be reaching up and maybe falling.

Poet: Is this all right?

Little Old Lady: Yes, it seems just fine. Nu, you were counting?

Young Man: Yes.

Poet: I never liked three, would four be all right with everyone?

Young Woman: It's O.K. with me.

Little Old Lady: Three, four, it's all the same.

Young Man: O.K., but you count this time.

Poet: One, two, three . . .

> *Enter Old Man. Also with a noose.*

Old Man: Solid old tree, well I guess you'll do for me this time.
(*Oblivious to others. Gets noose ready.*)
Oh!

Little Old Lady: Again!

Old Man: Yes, she didn't want me. She laughed. I can't help it.
So she's not the only one. But I miss her. I can't stand it anymore.

Little Old Lady: So why talk? Here's a place. With talking we've had enough.

Old Man: (*to Young Woman*) But you, why? I thought if anyone, a lovely young girl; there's always a place in this world for someone . . .

Young Man: (*to Poet*) See? Male chauvinism in the worst extreme.

Old Man: Well, your manners certainly haven't improved.

Little Old Lady: So bad his manners aren't.

Old Man: But why?

Young Woman: You really want to know?

Poet: Yes, we're listening Ellen.

Young Man: (under his breath) Do we have a choice.

Young Woman: I, I opened up to my shrink, psychiatrist that is.

Old Man: But that's good. It's the first step to being better.

Young Woman: I told him everything, about my thoughts, how what sex means to me, about the boys I've known, what I've always wanted to do, what I think about at nights.

He said I had a dirty mind.

Poet: You never talked like that to me.

Young Man: Lucky for you she didn't. You'd write a poem to dirty minds.

Old Man: So that's the way therapy works. I always wondered.

Young Woman: Oh, it's really wonderful. You should try it. It's really very good for you.

Little Old Lady: Me, I never knew about such things. You weren't happy, you ate.

Young Man: Ahem. Do you mind? Is everyone set?

Old Man: I think I'm all ready over here.

Young Woman: Me too.

Little Old Lady: More set I'm not going to get.

Poet: Ready when you are.

Young Man: We were going to go on four, is that all right with you?

Old Man: Four, sure. But since there are five of us, why not five?

Young Man: Five?

Poet: O.K.

Young Woman: Sure.

Little Old Lady: It's my birthday today.

Poet: Why congratulations.

Young Woman: Happy birthday.

Old Man: Many happy returns.

Young Man: Happy birthday. Now . . .

Young Woman: How old are you?

Little Old Lady: Sixty-six. You're all very kind.

Old Man: Why it's the least we can do.

Poet: Oh, let's sing happy birthday. Happy birthday to you, happy birthday to you . . .

Young Man: Enough.

Little Old Lady: Sixty-six, and who remembers my birthday? Not a card. From my son, the homosexual, a note do I get? From my sister in Peoria, you think a call maybe? Not a word. Nothing. Like I didn't even exist. But it's all right. When I'm gone they'll know how I loved them.

Old Man: That's very sad. But you certainly have my heartfelt congratulations. I should only live so long.

Young Man: Can we go ahead?

ALL: Yes.
   Alright, sure.
   Let's get on with it.

Young Man: One, two, three . . .

Poet: I only hope it doesn't hurt too much.

Old Man: I'll tell you. I know from experience; just smile. It only hurts if you're laughing.

Young Man: We've had enough interruptions. I just hope no one comes along now.

ALL: Me too.

    Black out

THE END

Princess

First Excuse me, I saw your sign there: "If you've lost your dog inquire within"?

Second Yes, that's right.

F Well, I've lost my dog.

S Gee, that's too bad. You've come to the right place though. If anyone can help you, we can.

F I hope so. I'm lost without her. I miss . . .

S Can you describe him?

F Her. How can I describe her? She's beautiful—about so high, black, with a white chest. Real friendly. Everyone on the block can tell you . . .

S What breed?

F Breed? Labrador maybe. Maybe greyhound. A little bit of both, though she doesn't look like either. She's very affectionate—don't mind her barking. She'll come to you if you just call. Princess (*whistles*) Princess (*whistles*) Princess (*breaks down*).

S I'm sorry it's affected you so much. People get so worked up about their dogs you know. I wish I could help. That's the nice thing about this job, when I can help someone find his dog. It's heart-warming, satisfying. It makes the job seem worthwhile. You don't get into a job like this for the money. Nope. It's the satisfaction of seeing owner and dog reunited. I tell you I get such a warm glow all over when we bring the dog in and he'll leap all over his master, licking him and you think, well, that's good. And the tears of joy. Why sometimes it's almost embarrassing.

   (*more sobbing by F*)

   And it's funny, it's not the small children who're always the happiest. Nope, it's the old folks. Sometimes they're near shock when we bring in their dog. You'd think it's all they have. And the dog'll be licking and whimpering and they won't hardly move. Nearly shock.

   Of course sometimes they don't move cause it's not their dog. We make mistakes, too, you know. Don't look at me that way; if it's an honest mistake it's an honest mistake. But we go back and keep looking. That's the bad part of the job, when we can't find their dog. Of course we'd always like to get them back together, and it's frustrating when we can't. Leaves a bad taste in your mouth. Some folks'll just keep haunting this place, week after week. It tears me up to see 'em sitting there, never giving up hope. When after all, we know we're not going to find their dog.

(*sobbing throughout*)

Though I guess they don't really expect us to find 'em anymore. They're just not admitting it to themselves. And you don't know how it hurts me to tell them that they really can't keep coming back. After all, the waiting room gets crowded sometimes and, gee, it just gets on my nerves. I mean someone there every day looking at me like it's my fault. We're trying. I tell you, we're trying. But what can you do, manufacture 'em out of thin air? I ask you.

Here, use my handkerchief.

F   Thank you. (*whistles*) Princess, Princess (*sobs*). Oh God, running across the lawn in the sunlight, chasing squirrels, and she'd run over to me and nuzzle up. And when I came home she'd be so excited she'd jump up on me ... (*barely restraining sobs*).

S   Yes, that's dogs for you. No consideration, always muddying you up. Course I don't have one, but it's not cause of that. No, it's cause if I had one, well I'd probably lose it, or it'd lose me, or it'd run away and then I'd be just like you, having to come in here, sitting on that side of the desk, sobbing. I've got enough troubles without that. It's bad enough having to hear folks cry everyday without having to end up being the one crying, too.

F   But, but Princess, do you think you can help me find her?

S   I'll look in my card file. Here.

F   She could be hungry. Lost and no one to look after her. Whining in some back alley. Or maybe she's been hurt ...

S   Now, black dog. All black. Primarily black. Would you say she's primarily black?

F   Yes. She's got a white chest, right along here, and white paws. But if you saw her you'd say she's a black dog.

S   Mmmmm (*searching in file*)

F   She's a little old, so she's got some gray. Especially here around the chin. But she's still alert. I mean dogs don't get old like we do. They don't get senile or anything.

S   Yes, primarily black. And under ones with white chests I've got beagles. Could she be a beagle?

F   No. What do you take me for? A beagle?!

S   Bloodhound?

F   No.

S   Collie? Dachshund? German shepherd? Pincer? Sheepdog? Saint Bernard?

F   No.

S   We've got four St. Bernards. They aren't even black. Personally I don't think they're lost at all. No one ever seems to claim a St. Bernard. I think their owners lose them on purpose. You know, someone gets a dog, and they think they're going to love him always, and it's just what they want, and then things change and they realize how much it's going to eat. Have you ever seen a St. Bernard eat? Like a horse? Unh unh. No horse I ever saw ate like that.

F   Please, could you keep looking. Is that all the ones you have now? Are you sure?

S   No, no, there's still terriers. And a toy poodle. You know it's funny how few poodles we get. Now you think that since so many people don't like them, like you, I can see you don't think much of them. Just a silly kind of dog. Well, me too. Too high strung. Like a toy. We'll, you'd think we'd get lots of them here—like with the St. Bernards. But nope, nary a one. I guess people who choose them must really love them a lot

     (*sobbing*)

to get them in the first place. They know their own mind, and if they're living in some small apartment, well, it's probably all they've got. But they get so protective. I've seen them here sometimes when the owners come in. Oh they say they're looking for another lost dog, but I know they're just showing off that they haven't lost theirs. And those dogs are so spoiled.

F Poodles . . . ? And that, that's the last?

S No, after that we've got mongrels. Say, didn't you say yours was a mongrel?

F Crossbreed. But yes, can you look there?

S Let's see — a real small one, eh?

F No, no medium size. About so.

S Right. Short-haired?

F No, longhaired. Or medium haired I guess. Look, I said like a cross between a labrador and a greyhound. Can't you imagine that?

S I'm doing the best I can.

F I'm sorry. It's just that you're my last hope. If you can't find her I don't know where to look anymore.

S Let's see, let's see. Here's one. Answers to the name "Harold".

F Harold?

S Could she have answered to the name Harold?

F Not likely. But maybe. What's it say.

S Just like you described, a puppy, and . . .

F No, not a puppy. Old. She's old now. That can't be her.

S I'll keep looking.

F For a while I'd given up hope. But then one day I heard someone call his dog a lot like I used to, and I thought (*whistles*) here Princess, (*whistles*) here Princess. And I just started crying (*sobs*). I've been frantic ever since. I have to find her. Princess, Princess, . . .

S Well, I think I can say that she's definitely not in our files.

F Oh God, no! . . .

S But wait, please, stop, don't cry, please, there's still a chance. Please.

F How!? A chance? No, not now. (*cries*)

S   Yes, yes, please. Look, look here. See this, it's our missing dogs file. You put a card in here for a small fee, and then we broadcast once a day for anyone who finds a dog to notify us. Everyone knows to tell us when they find a dog. And, look, hey, please stop crying, you'll be sure to find her. There's been lots of people come in here and not find their dog right off and a few days later or maybe a week or two weeks, or maybe even longer we get their dog showing up. Some kid'll find it and bring it in. You'll see. That's right. Calm down.

F   There's still a chance?

S   Yes, yes, sure, there's a real good chance. Now I've got all the information except where you lost her. Can you tell me that?

F   I don't rightly know, cause she used to roam a lot. I live over on Oak St. I guess you better put that down. Somewhere around Oak St.

S   All right. And when did you lose her?

F   Let me think. It was . . . it was eleven years ago.

S   Eleven . . . What!? Eleven years ago!?

F   Yes, I'm absolutely certain. I was 17 at the time. I looked real hard for her then, for a long time. But I just gave up. And then I heard that whistle, like I told you, and it reminded me, and your sign said inquire here if you've lost your dog . . .

S   And you expect us to find her for you?

F   Look, it's my last chance. I'm desperate!! Can you understand? I love her. Princess, Princess. Oh, where can she be . . . Princess . . . (*breaking down*).

S   But after all these years, I mean . . .

F   But your sign said, if you've lost your dog inquire within. I can't stand being without her anymore. I could never get another one. It wouldn't be the same, and besides, she learned to like me when I was a kid, and I know that it wouldn't be easy for a dog to learn to like me now. I'm not so loveable anymore. And you're my last chance.
    (*pause*)
How come you're not writing?

- S Eleven years? All right, I'll write it down. Look, you see here, eleven years. Does that say what you told me? I mean, I wouldn't want to make a mistake.
- F And you'll broadcast that out? Everyone'll be looking for her?
- S No, we broadcast that any lost dog should be brought to us. So everyone'll know we're the place to bring a lost dog. And if yours shows up as one of the lost ones we'll call you.
    Are you sure you wouldn't be interested in getting another dog? There's lots that are brought to us that never get claimed. One of them would be sure to make you happy. How about a nice beagle? Or a St. Bernard?
- F Another dog wouldn't be the same. Princess was the dog of my youth. How could I ever replace you?
    You know I finally realized that, and that's when I started looking for her again.
- S Well, Princess is down in our files. I sure hope you find her.
- F You've been awfully kind. You don't know how this has encouraged me. I'm really grateful.
- S Glad to be of help.
- F And you'll call me just as soon as she's found?
- S Just as soon.
- F O.K. (*goes off, whistles*) Here Princess. (*whistles*) Here Princess.

Ralph

This monologue is actually for a man and a dog. A fierce, growling dog. Unfortunately, I've not been able to find one that will fiercely bark on cue and not attack. So I'll have to ask you to help me. Whenever you see me do this (*he gestures with his arm outstretched, fist clenched, thumb up*) I want you to bark. Really loud. Frighteningly. O.K.? Good, let's try it.

(*He gestures.*)

Oh no. Is that the best you can do? Let's try it again, really fierce this time. Come on.

(*He gestures, tries to get the audience as loud and involved as possible.*)

That's better. Now remember, every time I do this (*gestures, trying to fool the audience, then encourages them, waits till they respond*), you'll bark.

Ready?

(*All lines should be addressed to the audience as if it were the dog. The letter **B** indicates a place where a gesture calling for a bark is needed.*)

*   *   *   *   *   *

(*Scene: A city street. A man is walking along, humming or whistling a tune. He is stopped, indeed terribly startled by the fierce barking of a dog.* ***B***)

God damn dog! God damn dog!
Hey, can't you keep your God damn dog locked up?

(*Dog is still growling.* ***B***)

I can't take a walk without a dog trying to bite my leg off. Hey! keep your dog tied up why don't you, he scared me half out of my wits.

(*Every time he yells the barking grows louder.* ***B***)

O.K., O.K., nice doggy, here poochie, nice doggie, let me by now, that's right just pretend I'm not here, and I'll walk right by.

(*He starts to walk by – barking and growling are much louder and fiercer.* ***B***)

Ralph

Hey, hey dog, I'm going back, see? — go out to take a walk and I can't even stay on this side of the street. I go for a walk, try to settle my nerves, feel all great and relaxed and I'm scared half to death. It's not like I'm doing this just to get to the other side of the block. No; a little relaxation is all I want and I can't even get through two blocks.

Damnit. This is the side of the street I'm walking on. Why should I move over?

(*He advances a bit, dog growls low and throatily.* **B**)

O.K. dog. I got you, you want this side; so do I.

(*He begins to circle the dog [audience] as if he were a participant in a dog fight. Throughout there are appropriate growls from the dog – and from the man.*)

C'mon. Want to smell me, eh? What's wrong you won't leave the driveway, huh? Only to attack? Is that it? It's your home you're defending? Well, what's to say it's yours. This is a city, dog, and no one, dog or man, gets a private home here. No, if I can't have a bit of peace here, you sure can't either.

Yeah, c'mon, a little closer, I'll strangle your furry rank smelling doggy neck. Hey, you think I don't have teeth? Try me dog, try me. What's wrong, I'm too much like a dog for you, eh? You're not used to someone as big as me growling back? Well your home my ass.

(*He advances – dog barks incredibly fiercely and sounds as if he is ready to attack.* **B B**)

O.K., O.K., you come out to meet me. Here, I'll leave you all over the sidewalk if you don't back down. Just the two of us for this spot, only which of us is going to back down? Not me dog. All I've got are these walks; cooped up all day in a building, all night in a dark room with a bed and a chair and the walls streaked from the rains last winter, and most of the time it's so smoggy I don't even want to go out, so this is it dog. These walks are it. They're the only things that make me feel even a bit human, and you're not going to take them away from me. Not you or any of your unleashed little friends. These walks are it And I like this street, see. Nice trees, a bit of lawn, and it's a decent day, no goddamn dog is going to stop me from trying to pry back a tiny bit of my sanity from the universe. YOU HEAR DOG!

(*Loud barking in response.* **B**)

You hear?! Hey, is it because of your bone? I just want to walk out here, real peacefully, quiet, you see, just humming a tune, trying to shift some peace out of this day. And you won't let me do it dog. Do you hear? You won't let me have any peace. You too!

(*B*)

Well dog, I can be pushed just so far. Just so far. Then no farther. And you've pushed me; no one else has even said anything to me. No, nothing I could take exception to, no insults, no pushing, all of them just quietly making my life miserable till you started barking.

(*Man barks at dog – dog barks back.* ***B***)

Most meaningful conversation I've had in ages. Grrrr.

At least I know where you stand. Yeah and me too. And now you don't have a dog pack with you, do you? You think I don't have a pack too, huh? Well, let me tell you, I'm not lonely. Oh no, I've got me plenty of friends. And I talk to them too. Only we don't communicate with each other quite as well as you and I do. That's the problem; I've got plenty of friends, but I don't have any god damn enemies. That's right dog. No enemies, no one I can really hate, no one – that's right, come a little closer—

(*He makes a sudden lunge –* ***B B*** *– the dog retreats and makes horribly menacing sounds. He laughs deeply and throatily.*)

—no damn enemies like you, dog. Nobody I could strangle like you mutt.

Hey, what's this, a nameplate for you on the fence—Ralph?! Ralph? ha ha ha ha ha hahahahaha ... Ralph! what a rotten name. (*Dog whimpers.*) You poor son of a bitch, I'd whimper too if someone gave me a name like that and I had to chew my bones all day long under a sign that said "Ralph" on it. Ralph! Ha! Here fella. Let's be friends, what do you say, eh Ralph? All right?

(*He advances with outstretched hand – sounds of fierce barking and teeth and jaws snapping.* ***BB***)

ALL RIGHT! I gave you a chance, I tried to be your friend and you nearly bit my hand off. Well that's it Ralph, you're a dog, a rotten dog and I'm walking here and you're backing down, you hear? Me, it's gonna be me that's king dog here. Me – two males, just sniffing each other and there isn't room for the two of us, eh? Well, I don't want your female bitch, I just want to walk here and tear some shred of peace from this day and you keep barking at me and you're making me lose my temper do you hear, Ralph? Do you hear? I'm not going to back down! I'll rip my tranquility right out of your side! I will! I'm not a violent person, but I'll wash myself in your dog's blood if you don't back down. I will Ralph. I will!

(***BB*** *He advances a step toward the now fiercely barking dog. the dog leaps at him. There is a fierce struggle [in mime] – the dog going for the man's throat, and the man trying to fend the dog off, finally trying to strangle the dog.*)

I'll kill you.
Die you dog.
It's you or me now.

(*Finally he pins the dog back and puts the death grip on his throat, the dog is whimpering.*)

Die damn you, die! Die dog. Now!

(*Dog gives a last shuddering whimper and expires. The man is kneeling where he has strangled the dog. He gets up sometime during the next speeches.*)

Hah! Dead—you're dead dog.
Two males met here, and the stronger one won. That's right, the bigger, stronger, smarter one won. And that was me! Me!
You're dead Ralph. Dead! And you know what I've won? Huh? You know? I can walk the streets now. This street. And no dog is going to scare me! No sir. No barking dog is going to interrupt my dreams. I can walk proud and not have to jump at growling around a corner. That's cause I won, and you're dead, and this here is my street if I want it.
Look at this, my shirt's ripped, I'm even bleeding. I'm not saying you didn't fight well. You fought hard. But I fought harder Ralph. Here, I'll put you under your name plate near the fence. Survival of the fittest old Ralphie.
Damn, what a mess. I sure am dirty. I'll have to go home now and get all cleaned up. I wonder if there'll be time for maybe a walk before dinner.

(*He shuffles out.*)

MY FIGHT with the ALLIGATORS

based on a true story

Characters

*HERMAN MELTOWN   * indicates major character
*LOUISE MELTOWN   his wife
*MARTY   their son
RODRIGUEZ   the foreman
*FINKEL
*CARNEY THE SWIMMER
JOE   Herman's first partner
BOY
MOTHER
VENDOR
VOICE of ALLIGATOR
SECRETARIES (3)

Approximate running time 50 minutes.

Scene 1

BOY: Mommy, Mommy, I wanna, I wanna . . .

MOTHER: No. You're not going to have an alligator.

BOY: But mommy, mommy, whaaaa . . .

MOTHER: No, really Sidney, no.

BOY: Whaaaaa (full fledged tantrum).

MOTHER: Stop it! Stop it this instant Sidney. I said stop it.

BOY: Whaaaa . . .

MOTHER: Look Sidney, how about a nice ice cream cone?

BOY: Whaaaa . . .

MOTHER: A candy bar? Look, a wind-up little man? A toy howitzer? A koala bear? A puppy? A horse?

BOY: I wanna alligator, I wanna alligator . . .

MOTHER: Sidney! Will you stop it. Please Sidney. Oh all right, I'll give you the damned alligator.

(goes to vendor)

VENDOR: Get your alligators. Red hot alligators. Straight up from Florida. Nice new shipment here. Get your alligators. Hey lady, you wanna alligator? Huh? Make a nice pet. Eat almost anything. Very quiet. Easy to housetrain.

MOTHER: How much are they?

VENDOR: $35.

MOTHER: WHAT!

VENDOR: But for you a special deal. Only $27.50 . Look, I'll give you the best of the bunch. Yeah, that little one. Nice shiny skin. Alert, eh? Sharp tongue. You'll love him lady.

BOY: Oh mommy, that's the one, that's the one I want. Look, he loves me already. Look mommy, look . . .

MOTHER: Here. Well, take it from him Sidney. You don't think I'm going to touch it do you?

VENDOR: You won't regret it lady. You got a real nice alligator there. Just make sure he gets plenty of water.

BOY: Oh thank you mommy, thank you . . .

Scene 2

HERMAN: And so, many times over, in every part of this great Metropolis, this great city that is New York, USA, began the story of MY FIGHT WITH THE ALLIGATORS.

I musta been about 33 or so when it all started. The big craze about buying alligators. Stupidest damn thing I ever heard of when I read about it in the papers. O.K. I know a puppy's hard to keep in the city. But at least you can take it for a walk. It'll talk to you. But an alligator. What's it gonna do? No personality. Or at least I thought so then. Yeah, it's easy to housetrain. Only craps once a week. Brother. Not real friendly I thought.

Then we started reading about them escaping and all. In the papers. Didn't think too much about it then..

Scene 3

SECRETARY 1: Hello, Health Department. May I help you please? Yes, yes, . . . , yes . . . you got a what? Alligators? How the hell do I know what to do with an alligator. Flush it down the toilet for all I care. Crazy goddamn city.

SECRETARY 2: Sanitation Department. Mr. O'Reilly? About what please? Alligators? You kidding me mister ? Oh, Mr. Gomez, I'm so sorry. Certainly, I'll connect you right through.

Hey Mabel. Catch this. Line 14 . Gomez talking to the boss. Says he's got alligators in the sewers. No really.

SECRETARY 3: Office of the Mayor of New York. May I help you please? Mr. O'Reilly, Sanitation Director . Yes, I'll put you through.

(files nails)

Yes, Mr. Mayor. The National Guard? I don't have that number here. Shall I call you back?

Scene 4

HERMAN: Well, apparently there were all these alligators running loose in the sewers. Big ones, too. Feeding on rats and whatever floated free in that maze of cess pits under the city. Mayor wanted to call out the National Guard. Maybe toss in a few bombs. O'Reilly said a few bombs and the whole system would crack apart.

National Guard nixed it anyway. Lieutenant General Farquhar said he wasn't sending any of his men down a sewer hole in that sewer hole of a city to tramp around in the crap and slime so's they could get bit by alligators. Wasn't part of their training. Mayor tried to convince him it was a communist conspiracy. Using the sewers for hideouts. And the alligators as messengers. Sort of an underwater equivalent of carrier pigeons. General Farquhar told him to shove it.

Well, the mayor wanted to let it ride. You know, maybe next winter it'll freeze over and they'd all die. O'Reilly said maybe.

Then O'Reilly called him back. Turns out alligators are coldblooded. Anyway, the sewer system never freezes over. And the men from his sewer division were getting pretty upset.

Scared the hell out of them stepping on an alligator in the dark. How would it look election time that the mayor wouldn't authorize a few measly bucks to get rid of alligators and Joe Shmoe lost a leg in the sewers?
So the mayor says finally O.K. Get some of the unemployed bums in the city to work on it. Enough of 'em collecting welfare. Kill two birds with one stone. And if one of 'em gets eaten down there, after all those alligators get hungry, well, that's one less mouth bitching about how little they get paid on welfare.

That's where I come in.

Scene 5

LOUISE: Herman, get a job.

HERMAN: You get a job. I tried.

LOUISE: You tried. You think I could get a job if you can't?

HERMAN: Exactly.

LOUISE: Marty needs a new pair of pants. And a winter coat. You gonna let your son go to school like that?

MARTY: Mommy, can I have a nickel to buy a pencil? All the other kids at school get pencils. Huh?

LOUISE: Go away, mommy and daddy are talking seriously.

MARTY: Aw mommy, just a nickel.

LOUISE: Not now Marty baby. (MARTY goes) You want him to grow up with no education? Not even a pencil?

HERMAN: Louise, please, you know I've done everything I can. I've applied for every job I could find in the paper in the last 4 months. The employment office says I haven't got any skills. No skills. I'm strong, aren't I? I'm willing to work. You know I'm no bum Louise. Don't you? I'll put in as good a day's work as the best of 'em. I'm no slacker. You wouldn't of married a bum, would you?

LOUISE: Oh Herman, Herman, of course not. And I love you still. Despite the fact you haven't brought in any pay for 47 weeks.

HERMAN: There just aren't any jobs. I swear, there just aren't any jobs.

LOUISE: Maybe I could get a job. As a waitress in one of those fancy places downtown.

HERMAN: Oh, God. Please, Louise, no. I've seen them waitresses, two years on they get hardened. Pretty soon they're turning tricks. No, it makes you bad. Give me a chance. Please. Something'll show up.
Well, something did.

Scene 6

LOUISE: Hello honey. Beautiful day, isn't it? I'll be with you in a minute.

HERMAN: Great. (sarcastically)

LOUISE: Hello, Herman.

HERMAN: I got some news.

LOUISE: What? About a job?

HERMAN: Yeah, down . . .

LOUISE: Oh, wonderful!

HERMAN: Yeah, wonderful. Down at the employment office. They're checking out everyone who comes in to collect unemployment. Offering them a job, or they say they'll take you off the rolls.

LOUISE: But that's O.K. You want a job.

HERMAN: Yeah, hunting alligators.

LOUISE: What?

HERMAN: Hunting alligators.

LOUISE: But there aren't any alligators in New York. Alligators live in the tropics or something. Where it's warm. Like Florida.

HERMAN: That's what I said.

LOUISE: You don't mean we have to move to Florida? Herman, I don't want to leave New York. I know it's a lousy city, but it's always been my, our home. All our friends, our families.

HERMAN: Don't worry. We don't have to leave New York. Not even this neighborhood. Probably they're right here.

LOUISE: Herman . . . what are you talking about?

HERMAN: The alligators. Right here. Underneath us. In the sewers. Thousands of them. Damn spoiled New York kids bought alligators. As pets. Flushed 'em down the toilet. They want me to go hunting them.

LOUISE: Wait . . . What? You mean there's alligators in the sewers? Right here? Underneath us?

HERMAN: Yeah, probably.

LOUISE: I knew this city stank. I knew it was a hell-hole. Dirty. And crazy. But alligators. No, I don't believe it. Ha ha ha. It's a joke. Oh Herman. Ha ha ha.

HERMAN: (sarcastically) Ha ha. So look at your last welfare check. I told them what they could do with their alligators. Me and about 40 other guys down there. No one would take the job. Now we really are broke.

LOUISE: Herman (imploringly). You mean it's for real?

HERMAN: Yeah, it's for real. I may be broke, but I'm not going to risk my life down in those sewers chasing 15 foot alligators. No way.

(enter MARTY)

MARTY: Mommy, mommy . . . oh, hi daddy. Mommy, all the kids are going down to ride on the subways and take the ferry to Staten Island. Teacher says I need to get your permission to go, too. Mrs. Rosen is going to show us all about the subway, and the boat and all. Huh, huh, I can go can't I? It'll only cost 50¢.

HERMAN: Marty, I'm afraid not. We just don't have 50¢ to spare.

MARTY: But mommy.

LOUISE: I'm afraid daddy's right.

MARTY: Oh, mommy. Why can't I? Please . . .

HERMAN: Maybe next time. Go off to your room now and play with those nice cardboard boxes I brought you. See if you can make a fort. I'll be in in a little while.

MARTY: O.K. daddy. (exits)

HERMAN: Not even 50¢ for a subway ride and going out on the ferry.

LOUISE: And next week we won't even have this check.

HERMAN: I gotta take it, don't I ?

LOUISE: Oh Herman, I don't want you to. Down in those sewers. Who knows what you'll find.

HERMAN: Looks like I don't have much choice.

LOUISE: Herman . . .

HERMAN: Don't worry honey. I'll manage. And I'll be a good alligator hunter. I tell you. If they're going to pay me to kill alligators they're going to get their money's worth.

Scene 7

HERMAN: So that's how it all began. Went down the next morning. Right away they give me some hip boots and a flashlight. Big son-of-a-gun flashlight. Floats, too. And they sent me down with some guy who said he knew how to shoot a shotgun.

(climbing down sewer ladder from manhole)

JOE: You got that light secure ?

HERMAN: Yeah, it's secure. Hey, watch where you're pointing that gun.

JOE: Oh, yeah, sorry. (in the sewer now)

HERMAN: My name's Herman. What's yours ?

JOE: Joe.

HERMAN: Well, put 'er there Joe. I guess we'll be working together for awhile so we might as well be buddies.

JOE: Guess so.

HERMAN: Hey, you aren't nervous are you ?

JOE: Nyaahh. Just a bit edgy. Hey, get that light over here. What was that noise ?

HERMAN: Where ?

JOE: There, there, what is it ?
BLAM BLAM BLAM (shoots shotgun)

HERMAN: What the hell are you doing ?

JOE: Did I get it ?

HERMAN: Get what ?

JOE: The alligator.

HERMAN: That was no alligator.

JOE: What ?

HERMAN: As they say in the shows, that was no alligator, that was my wife.

JOE: Very funny. Very funny. Look, just keep that light in front of me.

HERMAN: Hey Joe, are you sure you know how to handle a shotgun? Didn't seem like it just then.

JOE: Oh, yeah, sure. You just keep that light over there.

HERMAN: Hey, you're dropping the barrel in the water.

JOE: Huh? Oh yeah.

HERMAN: You never shot a shotgun before, did you?

JOE: What?

HERMAN: I said, you never shot one of those things before.

JOE: So ?

HERMAN: So!!

JOE: Just keep that light over there. Look. BLAM BLAM BLAM

HERMAN: What the hell you shooting at ? Calm down will you ? Look, we better stop and figure this out.

JOE: What ?

HERMAN: How many shells they give you?

JOE: Shells. I don't know. A handful. Maybe 10.

HERMAN: And you've already shot 6 of 'em.

JOE: Look! BLAM BLAM BLAM BLAM

HERMAN: Holy Mother of God, what are you doing? There aren't any alligators in the ceiling. Stop it will you? That shot'll ricochet all over us. Look, that's ten gone anyway. Let's get back up to the top.

So I finally got him out of there before he killed both of us. Turns out he never shot anything bigger than a spitball before. Thought it would be neat to try a shotgun.

Joe wasn't cut out for hunting alligators. A few more sessions and he started to drink. He began to see alligators everywhere. Even in the subway, or his apartment. With all the noise he made in the sewers, though, we never did see a real one. Finally they had to take him off.

So they decided to teach me how to shoot.

Scene 8

LOUISE: Hello honey. How was it today?

HERMAN: Joe got fired. Rodriguez says they're going to teach me how to shoot. One of those shotguns. Says I'm the only man he can trust down there not to get lost or blow my own head off.

LOUISE: Herman? You shoot? But you've never even been close to a gun before.

HERMAN: Except for that time I got mugged on 44th St.

LOUISE: Herman, I'm afraid.

HERMAN: Look, we work in pairs. One guy on a flashlight, one shooting. With the yo-yos I've gotta work with I'd rather be the one holding the gun. When I was working with Joe is when you should have been afraid.

LOUISE: Are you sure?

HERMAN: Yeah, I'm sure. Look, it's not that dangerous. I still haven't seen an alligator. No one I met has either, though word has it that some guy up on 58th St. bagged two of 'em already.

Look, it's a position of some responsibility. Handling the gun. And Louise, it *is* safer.

LOUISE: If you're *sure*.

Scene 9

HERMAN: So Rodriguez taught me how to shoot. Ten minutes he taught me.

RODRIGUEZ: O.K., you hold it this way. With the barrel pointing away from you.

HERMAN: Look, I'm not an idiot.

RODRIGUEZ: Then you're the first one I've worked with that wasn't.

HERMAN: Go on.

RODRIGUEZ: Then you put it to your shoulder, like this, aim and fire. Do try to aim, will you?

HERMAN: Like this?

RODRIGUEZ: Already they've cut us down from 10 shells per man per day to 6 shells per day. If you guys would just aim once in awhile that'd be plenty. Look, don't worry. One shot'll probably be plenty. Maybe two. I don't know. I never shot an alligator before.

HERMAN: What!!??

RODRIGUEZ: I been hunting lots. Killed rats. And a possum. Blam, one shot and they're down. But an alligator's pretty big. Maybe two shots. Anyway, six shells is plenty. For three alligators. Maybe four if you guys would aim. Anyway, not one of my gang's got one yet. Murphy's gang up on the 50's has already got 4 . And I'm stuck with you yo-yos.

HERMAN: O.K., O.K. This how you hold it then?

RODRIGUEZ: Yeah, that's right. Then you aim.

HERMAN: Yeah, yeah, then I aim.

RODRIGUEZ: Then you pull the trigger. Once for every shot.

HERMAN: Hey, I can't.

RODRIGUEZ: That's because the safety's on. Here, that's a safety catch. Stops you from blowing off your own toes. Instead of your partner's.

HERMAN: Like this, then? BLAM BLAM BLAM

RODRIGUEZ: Help! You crazy son-of-a-

HERMAN: Sorry. I didn't know it was loaded.

RODRIGUEZ: Now you only got 3 shells left for today. Get on down there. Hey, Finkel, you, you hold Meltown's flashlight. And tie your shoelaces will you, so we don't have to drag you back up again when you trip over them down there.

HERMAN: Wait. That's all? I just pull the trigger? Hey, Rodriguez, that's no lesson. I knew that much from watching the movies.

RODRIGUEZ: And I ain't no teacher. Get on down there. You'll do just fine. Here, I'm giving you one of our best torch men. Finkel. You guys go on down there and bring me back an alligator.

HERMAN: Rodriguez (pleadingly) . . .

RODRIGUEZ: Get on down there.

HERMAN: But, but . . .
   (crawling down manhole ladder, after FINKEL)

RODRIGUEZ: And don't lose the flashlight again, Finkel, or we'll take it out of your pay. You hear?

HERMAN: Lose the flashlight? Finkel? Finkel? Where's the light?

   (manhole cover slams shut)

FINKEL: Yeah.

HERMAN: Will you turn the light on. Please . . .

FINKEL: Just a second. Ahhh. (click)

HERMAN: What ?

FINKEL: Had to fart.

HERMAN: Oh Lord. Can't smell it down here, anyway. Oh, for crying out loud, you can. What have you been eating Finkel?

FINKEL: Oh nothing special.

HERMAN: Look Finkel, you and I are going to be down here together for a while. Right? Get that light out of my eyes.

FINKEL: Sorry.

HERMAN: So we better trust each other. Right?

FINKEL: Yeah, I guess so.
I trust you.

HERMAN: I wish I could say the same. Here, stand close to me. Not that close. And keep that flashlight covering the ground ahead of us.

FINKEL: I don't see any ground.

HERMAN: Water, that is. The water ahead of us. Keep it going back and forth in an arc, so we can see the whole tunnel. You got it?

FINKEL: Yeah.

HERMAN: Not so fast. Back and forth slowly. You want to make us dizzy? That's right. O.K. let's start.

FINKEL: O.K.

HERMAN: What was that?

FINKEL: I farted. Big deal.

HERMAN: Look, the idea is to sneak up on these alligators. Quietly. We don't want to scare 'em away.

FINKEL: Yeah, yeah. O.K.

HERMAN: Try to hold it in.

FINKEL: O.K. but if you'd seen an alligator like I saw last week you wouldn't want to sneak up on 'em.

HERMAN: What?

FINKEL: I said, if you saw ...

HERMAN: I know what you said. I was just amazed you said it. I didn't know you knew so many words.

FINKEL: Ha ha. Big alligator. Size of a small car. Like one of them imported ones. Real sleek.

HERMAN: You say you saw ... You sure it wasn't a car? Lots of stuff floating around here you know.

FINKEL: If it was a car it sure knew how to snap it's hood and hiss at us. Big teeth too.

HERMAN:

FINKEL: You still want me to be quiet?

HERMAN: Big teeth.
  Yeah. We're paid to kill alligators, not chase them around the sewers. We'll take it real slow today.

FINKEL: Slow.

HERMAN: Yeah, slow. You got a watch.

FINKEL: Yeah.

HERMAN: What time is it?

FINKEL: 10:45 .

HERMAN: Let's get going.

So we started off. With all the guys pairing up to hunt alligators I had to get the only one whose farts were so bad you could smell them in a sewer. No one could stand Finkel. I didn't know that then. Rodriguez had palmed him off on me. Maybe it was a compliment. Thought I could handle him.

I never thought we'd get through that day. I needed a gas mask. I swore I'd never work with him again. I tell you, I swore it.

Scene 10

HERMAN: Listen, Rodriguez, I'm not going down with Finkel again.

RODRIGUEZ: What's wrong? He got through the whole day without losing his flashlight. No problem.

HERMAN: If you think ...

RODRIGUEZ: First time we didn't have to send someone down looking for him, too.

HERMAN: Well, I don't ...

RODRIGUEZ: You guys make a great pair.

FINKEL: (entering) Hi.

HERMAN: If you think that I'm ...

FINKEL: Well, I'm ready. Herman, I trust you.

HERMAN: Oh God.

RODRIGUEZ: You'll be fine. Go on down there.

(manhole slams shut)

HERMAN: FINKEL!

FINKEL: Yeah.

HERMAN: Turn on the light.

FINKEL: Yeah. (click)

HERMAN: You're the only guy I know who can stand in a sewer in the pitch black and not worry about it.

FINKEL: I hid in closets a lot when I was a kid.

HERMAN: Used to the dark, huh?

FINKEL: Yeah. Can see pretty well in it, too. Lots of carrots.

HERMAN: Carrots?

FINKEL: For my eyes. Lots of 'em. Helps you see in the dark.

HERMAN: Well, I like the flashlight *on*. Understand?

FINKEL: Yeah. I trust you.

HERMAN: And you can stop saying that.

FINKEL: Why? I do. Feels good down here. Knowing you can handle that gun.

HERMAN: Let's hope so. What's that?

FINKEL: An old log.

HERMAN: Huh?

FINKEL: An old log with bits of paper stuck to it.

HERMAN: You can see a log with bits of paper stuck to it?

FINKEL: Yeah.

HERMAN: I was talking about that rat or something on the ladder.

FINKEL: Oh. I'm used to them. Didn't even notice. I thought you meant that log down there. Looks a bit like an alligator.

HERMAN: Where?

FINKEL: Way down there.

HERMAN: Oh yeah. I can just barely make it out.

FINKEL: Told you I got good eyes.

HERMAN: You sure do. What time is it?

FINKEL: Nearly 10.

HERMAN: We should be near the intersection of 44th and 3rd Ave. You see a ladder anywhere?

FINKEL: There—down that tunnel.

HERMAN: Where?

FINKEL: There.

HERMAN: I see it now. Down this way?

FINKEL: Why not?

HERMAN: You sure?

FINKEL: No.

Scene 11

HERMAN: Well, we kept on for a couple days. I can't remember how many. Never saw an alligator. Nearly died from the kid's farts. But he had good eyes. I won't deny that. He sure could see. He even said he liked it down there. Turns out he hadn't got lost, those other times Rodriguez went looking for him. He just didn't feel like coming out.

(in sewer)

FINKEL: Yeah, carrots. Lots of 'em. And milk.

HERMAN: Milk?

FINKEL: Yeah, I drink about a gallon and a half a day.

HERMAN: Finkel. No one drinks a gallon and a half of milk a day.

FINKEL: And green peppers.

HERMAN: Why green peppers?

FINKEL: Why not? And at least one jar of pickles.

HERMAN: Finkel, I think I know why you fart so much.

FINKEL: Me, too. I'm nervous.

HERMAN: It ain't cause you're nervous ...

FINKEL: What's that?

HERMAN: What?

FINKEL: That noise.

HERMAN: What noise? Finkel, you got good hearing too?

FINKEL: Sssshhhh. The best. That's what the pickles are for. Look.

HERMAN: What?

FINKEL: If that ain't an alligator I'm the Virgin Mary.

HERMAN: Gulp. I think you're right. I think he sees us, too.

FINKEL: Yup. Sure looks like an alligator. (puts out light)

HERMAN: Finkel (sotto voce), Finkel. Where the hell's the light?

FINKEL: You want the alligator to find us?

HERMAN: Finkel, he can trace us by the smell of your farts. Get that light on. Where is he? There he is, there he is. Where's the safety catch? Finkel! Keep that light on.

FINKEL: My nose itches.

HERMAN: Use your other hand.

FINKEL: Good idea.

HERMAN: There it is (meaning the safety catch) (Click) Look at the size of that alligator. Finkel, you there?

FINKEL: Herman, I trust you.

HERMAN: Look at those teeth.

FINKEL: Herman, I trust you.

HERMAN: Finkel, he's coming this way.

FINKEL: Herman, I trust you.

HERMAN: Alligator, this is it. BLAM BLAM BLAM
(splashing noises)
Finkel, Finkel, did I get him?

FINKEL: Herman, I ...

HERMAN: Finkel, open your eyes.

FINKEL: Is it over?

HERMAN: Did I get him? Wait, is that him? Yes. BLAM BLAM He's getting away. Come on Finkel, let's go.

FINKEL: Yeah.
        (Break here if necessary.)

Scene 12

HERMAN: After awhile we got used to seeing more of them. It was getting to be summer, and they were more active. The sewer was getting more active generally. Warm weather was bringing out more rats, the odd possum and fish, and the stink was nearly suffocating. Still, you could smell Finkel's farts.

I'd been down there with Finkel for maybe 5 weeks. We'd seen, I don't know, maybe 4 maybe 5 alligators. I'd finally learned how to aim the damn gun. But still we hadn't bagged one. Rodriguez was getting suspicious. But as long as we showed up regularly, checked in at all the points on our route, and Finkel didn't get lost, he couldn't complain. No one else on our gang had got one either.

    (in the sewer)

FINKEL: What we need is someone to teach us how to track 'em.

HERMAN: What?

FINKEL: The alligators.

HERMAN: I know what you mean. How can you track an alligator in the sewer?

FINKEL: I don't know.

HERMAN: Of course not.

FINKEL: That's why we should have someone show us how.

HERMAN: What?

FINKEL: To track the alligators. The lore of the sewer. There must be someone.

HERMAN: As far as I know we're the first gang to ever hunt alligators under New York City. Probably the last, too.

FINKEL: We need someone to teach us how to track 'em.

Scene 13

HERMAN: Well, I started thinking about what Finkel said.

Louise, I'm home.

LOUISE: What? Oh hi. Take off those boots right there.

HERMAN: Sorry, I guess I forgot.

LOUISE: It's bad enough you smell like a sewer, you don't have to track it in, too.

HERMAN: I'm sorry. I'll just get cleaned up.

LOUISE: Sorry I lost my temper.

MARTY: Mommy.

LOUISE: Yes honey.

MARTY: Mommy, no one at school believes me when I tell them that Daddy hunts alligators.

LOUISE: Well, just you don't listen to them.

MARTY: They say I'm making it up.

LOUISE: You know you're not. Can't you smell that your Daddy's been down in the sewers?

MARTY: Yeah. But the kids say that's cause he sleeps in the gutter.

LOUISE: You know that's not true.

MARTY: Mommy, does daddy really hunt alligators in the sewers?

LOUISE: Yes.

HERMAN: (entering) What's this?

LOUISE: He says the kids are teasing him cause they don't believe you're really an alligator hunter.

MARTY: And Johnny says I'm starting to smell bad, too, daddy.

HERMAN: Look, Marty. It's true, I work in the sewers, under the city, every day. I go down there with my partner. Finkel. And we hunt alligators. There's nothing to be ashamed of.

MARTY: But how come you never kill any?

HERMAN: Well, we just haven't had a good clear shot yet. It's just the way it is.

MARTY: I don't believe you really hunt alligators. I think you just sleep in the gutters. (runs off crying)

LOUISE: Herman. He didn't mean it.

HERMAN: I'm going to have to get one.

LOUISE: What?

HERMAN: The kid's right. You take a job, you should do it right. What kind of alligator hunter am I? I've never got one. I'll have to bag one, bring home the skin to Marty. It's not right that he doesn't respect his father.

LOUISE: He didn't mean it.

HERMAN: No, he's right. And Finkel was, too. We're just novices down there splashing around. Scaring them off. We don't know any more about hunting alligators after two months down there than when we started.

We gotta consult an expert.

LOUISE: A what?

HERMAN: A expert. Someone who can tell us how to track alligators in the sewers.

LOUISE: But I thought this was the first time they ever had alligators down there.

HERMAN: Yeah. But some of the old-timers that've been working down there on repairs and stuff ought to be able to teach us something.

LOUISE: You think so?

HERMAN: I have to think so. Marty's got to have a reason to respect his father.

Scene 14

HERMAN: So I asked around. Finally found that there was a guy, just retired. They called him Carney the Swimmer. I called him up and Finkel and I went to meet him.

(park bench, sounds of pigeons)

CARNEY: Over 40 years in the sewers. Then they throw you out. Too old. No one else knows this system like I do. Every turn, the old catacombs, the dead ends, all them tubes too small to get into.

FINKEL: Yeah.

CARNEY: I used to swim up them. That's why they called me Carney the swimmer. Go places no one else would.
    Christ, kid, you stink.

FINKEL: Huh?

HERMAN: He farts.

CARNEY: 40 years in the sewers and I never smelled anything that bad. What do you eat kid?

HERMAN: Don't ask.

CARNEY: Well, you want me to tell you about the sewers you either hold it in, or move off kid.

HERMAN: Finkel, you better sit on that other bench.

FINKEL: O.K.

CARNEY: Forty years. You got a smoke?

HERMAN: Yeah, here.

CARNEY: Places no one else even knew about. Hey, you hear about that mugger, when all those girls disappeared? You know— must've been 20, maybe 25 years ago. They found the bodies in a crypt under 62nd St? Well, I was the guy found them there. Yeah. Looking for what was backing up the drains in that neighborhood. No one else could get in there. They call in old Carney the Swimmer. And there they were. Decomposing away. Six of 'em. You look sick. Here, have a drag.

HERMAN: I'll, ... I'll be O.K.

CARNEY: That's one thing, you got to have a strong stomach. No use hunting down there if you don't.

HERMAN: Usually I'm O.K.

CARNEY: Well, it's all in your footing. How do you guys walk down there?

FINKEL: Huh?

CARNEY: Show me, how do you walk?

HERMAN: You show him Finkel, I don't feel I can get up right yet.

FINKEL: O.K. (walks) Sorta like that.

CARNEY: There, that's what's wrong. You walk like you're on the street. Boy, you're *under* the street. You're in water up to your hips. You got to walk differently.

HERMAN: What do you mean?

CARNEY: Look, you can't be trying to find your footing each step. Those rotten bricks they put in a hundred, a hundred and fifty years ago down under the Bowery, covered with moss. Even if you don't slip on your ass you'll never get anywhere. You'll spend all your time looking for a foothold. Trying to get your balance.

FINKEL: Yeah.

HERMAN: So what do you do?

CARNEY: You gotta love the sewer. Get into it. Don't fight it. Ease in. Learn the feel of it. Close your eyes. Then slide along, like the drift of the current, like a candy wrapper, or a potato chip bag, easy, easy, drift along. You thinking? Don't—just *feel* it.

HERMAN: (closing his eyes) Yeah, sort of.

FINKEL: (closing his eyes) Yeah.

CARNEY: When you're down there it's the whole world. Just you. And them tunnel walls. Stooped? No don't stoop. Crouch, from the knees. Your ass getting wet? Don't worry. Easy, then slide, drift with it, just another piece of crap under New York, human crap, heading out for the ocean, one of those big drain holes, those huge mothers near the end of the Bowery, just drifting. You slide in. You become part of the sewer. Don't fight it.

HERMAN: (in a sweat) I gotta have a smoke.

FINKEL: (getting carried away) Yeah. I got it. Slide. Don't step.

CARNEY: Kid, you got promise. You, you got to shoot, so don't get carried away too much.

HERMAN: Don't worry.

CARNEY: The kid, here, like a seeing eye dog. You got a future kid.

HERMAN: Whew. That's a whole new ball game. I hope I can handle it.

CARNEY: Don't worry. You got the sense, you got the gun. The kid here will lead you fine. Won't you kid?

FINKEL: Yeah.

CARNEY: Tell the guys down at the depot that Carney the Swimmer's working with you. They'll give you all the help they can.

Scene 15

HERMAN: Yeah, all the help they can. Went down to the main depot to try to get some info about where these reptiles might be hiding in the system. And when we told them Carney the Swimmer sent us they laughed us out of there. Carney the Looney they said. Old nut, they said. They showed us all this new gear they had, radar like things, and said that Carney was just afraid of it. Never tried anything new after he was 30. An old nut.

Well, Finkel thought otherwise. He was happy after that. Said to come on, we didn't need their help. Carney'd taught him what was important.

(in sewer)

HERMAN: What the hell are you doing Finkel?

FINKEL: Gliding.

HERMAN: What?

FINKEL: Gliding with the current. Like a candy wrapper. Drifting.

HERMAN: Well get your ass back here and turn on that light so if you do drift up to an alligator I can see where to pick up your remains.

FINKEL: Like Carney said. You can sense the walls, the floor.

HERMAN: Just drift right there at my right shoulder. And stop farting!

FINKEL: Yeah.

HERMAN: Sorry. I think I'm a little nervous. All that talk about those decomposing bodies.
Stop farting!

FINKEL: Herman, there's an alligator around.

HERMAN: What?

FINKEL: I sense it. It's in this tunnel here.

HERMAN: Give me that flashlight. Finkel, that's a dead end.

FINKEL: Yeah, there's an alligator. Now, can you hear him?

HERMAN: Wait. Yes.

FINKEL: Come on.

HERMAN: There's no way out for him now. And I've still got all six shells.
Finkel, it's getting pretty narrow.

FINKEL: Yeah.

HERMAN: I better go ahead. Shine the light there.

FINKEL: O.K.

HERMAN: It's getting narrower.

FINKEL: Glide.

HERMAN: Put that light up.
   I can see it.

   (huge alligator looms up, hisses)

HERMAN: I think we got it backed into a corner. Finkel, come up closer, I'm still too far away. Might wound him and get him really mad.
   Finkel!?

FINKEL: Just glide.

HERMAN: Finkel, open your eyes! Shine that light …
   Oh oh. Well alligator. This really is it.

   BLAM BLAM BLAM

HERMAN: Finkel. Finkel!! I got him.

   (alligator thrashing and dying)

HERMAN: Wait, no, look, he's turned back over, starting to swim …
   Finkel, the light. Hold it still …

FINKEL: Herman, I trust you.

   BLAM

HERMAN: Yes! Yes! WE GOT HIM !

   (alligator definitely dead)

HERMAN: Finkel, we got him, we got him, our first alligator. Finkel!
   (embraces him)
   Christ you stink Finkel.

Scene 16

HERMAN: Rodriguez wouldn't let me keep the skin. Said they had to send it to headquarters to prove the kill. Boy was he proud of me. First in his gang to bag one. 18 feet. Big? But I got to keep the feet.

   See Marty? These are its feet. See. That's the first alligator your father's killed.

MARTY: Gee.

HERMAN: He was bigger, bigger than from here to the kitchen.

MARTY: Really? Daddy, can I keep them?

HERMAN: Sure, I brought them home for you. Take 'em to school and show your friends.

MARTY: Wow. Look Mom, he said I can take them to school.

LOUISE: I know. Now it's time for bed. Run off and get into your pyjamas.

MARTY: How big was it?

HERMAN: Run off to bed now. I'll come in in a minute and tell you a story.

MARTY: I want to hear about how you got the alligator again.

LOUISE: Run off to bed now. (MARTY leaves)
I'm glad. He's really proud of you.

HERMAN: Yeah, it's what he needed. And you?

LOUISE: Me, too. My killer.

Scene 17

HERMAN: After that Finkel and I got pretty good at it. Oh, it was no picnic. But we knew what we were doing. We got one maybe every other day or so.

Finkel wanted to see Carney again. For more pointers. I wasn't anxious to, but since it was what got him going the first time I felt I better go with Finkel.

(at park bench)

CARNEY: You guys again. Word's reached me you're getting a few.

FINKEL: Yeah.

HERMAN: How'd you hear?

CARNEY: I still got contacts down under.
How is it kid?

FINKEL: Like you said. You can sense it.

CARNEY: Good, good. And you?

HERMAN: Ahh, I settled down.

FINKEL: He's good. Best underwater shot in town.
Herman, I trust you.

HERMAN: Can it kid.

CARNEY: Yeah, they say you're good.

HERMAN: I'm O.K. Look, Finkel wants to get more advice.
You know. Like last time.

FINKEL: Yeah.

CARNEY: What's there to tell? Kid, you know all that stuff about gliding as well as I.

FINKEL: Nyaahhh.

CARNEY: If you've swum.

FINKEL: Huh?

CARNEY: It don't really count, I mean you can't really get the sense of it, till you've swum.
You swum yet?

HERMAN: Hey, you trying to get my partner drowned? Finkel, don't listen to him.
We're going.

FINKEL: (to CARNEY) Not yet. I still got the fear.

CARNEY: You got to conquer that. No, that ain't right. Not conquer. You got to learn not to fight it. When you're part of the sewer, part of the tunnels, when you're down there not *in* the current, but actually part of the current. Then, then, you know the sewer. Then you're really good.

FINKEL: Yeah?

CARNEY: Wait, wait for the feeling. When you know the time is ripe, go, go with it, with the slime and the muck, with the crap and the candy wrappers ... swim.
And you!

HERMAN: Huh?

CARNEY: You're important, too. You got to watch him. Stabilize him. Don't let him forget where you are. The greatest sewer system in the world. But don't let him get off away. He needs you.

FINKEL: Herman, I trust you.

Scene 18

HERMAN: Well, I'm not pretending I understood half of what Carney the Swimmer was getting at, but somehow something got through. And Finkel was getting better. Each day.
    (climbing down ladder into sewer)
    Look, Finkel. I went to my doctor, right? And I got a diet from him specially for you. Look Finkel. To stop farting. He says it's all that milk. And green peppers.

FINKEL: What?

HERMAN: Milk and green peppers. They make you fart.

FINKEL: So?

HERMAN: I'm trying to tell you. It's not pleasant. Look, give it a try. Here, put it in your pocket. Just for a week.

FINKEL: This the diet?

HERMAN: Yeah.

FINKEL: But there's no milk or green peppers on it. Or kidney beans.

HERMAN: Kidney beans? You eat kidney beans, too?

FINKEL: Yeah, keeps your smelling sharp. Got a great nose.

HERMAN: Kidney beans? For your smelling?

FINKEL: Yeah.

HERMAN: Just try it. Please. For a week.

FINKEL: I don't think so.

HERMAN: Please.

FINKEL: But no milk? No green peppers ...

HERMAN: That's the idea.

FINKEL: I don't think so.

HERMAN: Please, just give it a try.

FINKEL: Well ... maybe. Come on. Let's go.

HERMAN: You're in a hurry?

FINKEL: Not exactly. But I feel something.

HERMAN: Maybe today's the day you're going to swim. Oh, Christ what am I saying? Look Finkel, forget I said that. I like you. I don't want to see you drown.

FINKEL: Yeah, I got that feeling too. Today's the day I take the plunge.

HERMAN: Finkel, you know Carney's a bit of a nut. I mean, some of his advice has been good for you, I know. But you don't have to listen to everything he says.
    Just stay near me.
    You listening? I don't want you to get lost.

FINKEL: Herman, I trust you. (dives, splashing)

HERMAN: FINKEL !!!!
    Finkel, where'd he go? Where's the light? What, what's that noise?

(splashing from opposite direction)

HERMAN: Finkel, how'd you get off in that direction? You went that way. Finkel? Alligator?
    Where is it? Back up, back up, a little light from this manhole cover. Back up. Don't panic. I've shot lots of them.

    (alligator hisses, swishes its tail)

Come on alligator.

VOICE of ALLIGATOR: We're going to get you. You've hunted us, killed us. What have we done to you? We're the good alligators. We eat the rats. We're your friends. And you've hunted us. Fourteen of us gone already. I, I have been sent to end you now.

    (splashing, thrashing, HERMAN nearly in a trance)

HERMAN: No you don't alligator !!!!
BLAM BLAM BLAM
(surfacing near his left ear with splashing)

FINKEL: What happened?

HERMAN: HELP!
BLAM

FINKEL: Herman, I trust you.

HERMAN: Finkel. Finkel. Alligator. You, under water. Alligator.

FINKEL: Yeah, you got him. Good shot.

HERMAN: Alligator talking to me …

FINKEL: Great! You're finally on to them.

HERMAN: Said he was going to …

FINKEL: Me and the current, the sewer. You, you're on to the alligators.

HERMAN: Huh? Finkel, I'm getting out of here.
(starts to climb up to manhole)

FINKEL: It's O.K. (climbing up too) You're on to them now. We'll be the greatest ever.

HERMAN: Yeah.

Scene 19

HERMAN: I swore I'd quit then. Never again. Didn't go back. Nightmares.

VOICE of ALLIGATOR: I am the spirit of Alligators Past.

HERMAN: Louise!

LOUISE: What is it?

HERMAN: Alligators.

LOUISE: Calm down. You're a little overworked. That's all.

MARTY: Daddy, will you tell me about the time you went under 42nd St. and could hear the truck and everything and found the alligator resting on a ledge and …

LOUISE: Later Marty. Daddy's tired.

MARTY: Aw gee.

LOUISE: Later. (MARTY goes)

HERMAN: I'm cracking up.
(knock at door)
What's that?

LOUISE: Just someone at the door. Hello?

FINKEL: Herman there?

HERMAN: Finkel!?

FINKEL: Where you been?

HERMAN: I'm seeing alligators. All the time.

FINKEL: I can't work without you. Nearly got killed yesterday. Markowitz was shooting.

HERMAN: Markowitz??? He doesn't know a gun from a toilet bowl. Markowitz?

FINKEL: Yeah.

LOUISE: I better just leave you two.

FINKEL: Missus. Can you get him back? He's the best.

LOUISE: Herman?

HERMAN: Why me?

FINKEL: We're the best. Us two. Lady, no one can touch him with a gun. And when I'm with him I'm good tracking in the sewers. But I ain't anything without him. I'm even trying that diet you gave me. Herman, I trust you.

LOUISE: What's that smell. Marty?

HERMAN: It ain't Marty. It's Finkel. A lot of help that diet. Here, let me see it.
   Finkel, you really been following this? There's nothing here could possibly make you fart.

FINKEL: I told you I got a nervous stomach.

HERMAN: You really been following this? Nothing else?

FINKEL: Oh, a few candy bars.

HERMAN: What kind?

FINKEL: You know. Peanut clusters.

HERMAN: How many?

FINKEL: I don't know. Maybe two, three dozen.

HERMAN: Finkel. You can quit the diet.

FINKEL: You coming back?

HERMAN: I don't know Finkel.

FINKEL: Come with me to Carney the Swimmer.

LOUISE: Who?

HERMAN: Carney. An old crank.

FINKEL: He was the best in his time.

HERMAN: Maybe.

Scene 20

HERMAN: Yeah, I finally went to Carney.

CARNEY: Back again, eh. Kid, sit over there. What's wrong? You look nervous.

HERMAN: I'm seeing alligators.

FINKEL: Yeah, and he won't go down again.

CARNEY: That's good. Kid, you swum yet?

FINKEL: Yeah. It was good.

CARNEY: I knew you'd be O.K. Shooting, shooting's different. You, you reached the crisis point. You go back down and you'll be the greatest ever hunted an alligator in New York City. You stay up here, you're a washout. A has-been. Laughing stock. He hears alligators, they'll say.
   You want that?

HERMAN: No.

CARNEY: Sure you hear alligators. Cause you live with them. All day, under the Bowery, you can't even hear a truck sometimes, so quiet, and you begin to sense 'em, right?

HERMAN: Right.

CARNEY: Well, you're on to them then. You *know* alligators. I'll tell you, you weren't a born hunter. First time I saw you I knew that. Thought you'd never make it. But you learned. You learned. And now you're good. Could be the best, and you're backing out. You are The Alligator Man now! Like me, Carney the Swimmer. Go back down there and be the best.

FINKEL: Yeah.

HERMAN: I'll try.

CARNEY: And I'll tell you, now you're going back down. There's a spot, down by the Bowery. Third Ave. You got a map?

HERMAN: Yeah.

CARNEY: About there. Four pipes meet. A kind of whirlpool there. Deep. Maybe four feet, unless it's been raining, then it could be six, maybe seven. You'll know it. Off to the left, that's where McGregor hung himself. He was good, too, but he couldn't get past that crisis point. Best wrench man around. Took him twenty years, too. Not just a summer like you young ones. Then he cracked. Couldn't take it. Hung himself there.

They say it's bad luck there. Haunted. Don't believe any of that crap. You take the second pipe after the whirlpool. The second, understand?

HERMAN: Yeah.

CARNEY: Then go down. It slopes downward. Pretty fast, narrows a lot, too. Then you'll get to where there's no head room. You listening, kid?

FINKEL: Yeah.

CARNEY: Then you got to swim.

HERMAN: What!?

FINKEL: Yeah.

CARNEY: Keeps all but the best out. Probably hasn't been anyone up there since me, and that's five years ago.

    Then it widens, sort of like an underground cavern. And way back in there. That's where they'll be if they're anywhere.

HERMAN: Who?

CARNEY: The alligators. If they're anywhere, that'd be where they're hiding.

HERMAN: The alligators.

CARNEY: That'd be their nest, or my name's not Carney the Swimmer. Kid, you see he makes it there.

FINKEL: Yeah.

CARNEY: And you, you know the kid's going to go down there now. And you're the only gun that can protect him. Ain't no one else in this city that could.

FINKEL: Herman, I trust you.

HERMAN: Me?

CARNEY: You.

Scene 21

HERMAN: Louise. Louise I'm going now.

LOUISE: Bye dear.

HERMAN: Louise, you don't understand. This is the big day. I can't hold off Finkel any longer. We're going after the big ones.

LOUISE: It'll be fine honey. Don't worry.

HERMAN: I couldn't explain about the nest of alligators to her. I didn't even understand it myself. But I knew it was going to be there.

Scene 22

FINKEL: (climbing down ladder) Herman, I trust you.

HERMAN: Will you stop saying that? That's six times and we're not even down yet.

FINKEL: We're going to 3rd Ave.

HERMAN: To the nest.

FINKEL: Herman, I …

HERMAN: Will you please stop saying that! What'd you eat last night? That's the foulest smell I've… Finkel, what did you eat?

FINKEL: I been preparing. Getting my eyes and ears and nose ready. You know, milk, green peppers and …

HERMAN: Let's get going.
(they walk)
We must be getting close. You sense anything?

FINKEL: The current. Yeah. About a hundred, maybe a hundred and twenty yards up there's a whirlpool.

HERMAN: That must be it.

FINKEL: Yeah.
(they walk)

HERMAN: Must be it.

FINKEL: Yeah. Second pipe?

HERMAN: Second pipe.

FINKEL: It's starting to slope down.

HERMAN: Like Carney said. Not much more headroom. Finkel. We're going to have to swim now. I got the shells in the plastic bag. Finkel. You ready, too?

FINKEL: Herman, I trust you.

HERMAN: Finkel, I trust you.

(they dive — splashing and spluttering)

HERMAN: (whispering) Finkel. Finkel. This it?

FINKEL: Yeah. Neat.

HERMAN: Finkel, you O.K. ?

FINKEL: Yeah, had a little trouble with toilet paper in my eyes. Herman?

HERMAN: Yeah. It's vast.

FINKEL: You smell anything?

HERMAN: Finkel?

FINKEL: I mean alligators.

HERMAN: Yeah, they're here all right. Let's go along this wall. They're here all right.

FINKEL: Herman I ...

HERMAN: Shut up Finkel.

(huge alligator rising on its tail, sound of splashing)

VOICE of ALLIGATOR: Stop. Who would enter here? Who disturbs the nest of the alligators of New York City!? Who!?

HERMAN: HERMAN and FINKEL !!

VOICE of ALLIGATOR: Stop. Go no further. For in the nest of alligators shall you die.

HERMAN: BLAM BLAM BLAM

FINKEL: You got him.

HERMAN: Only three shells left. Let's get out of here.

FINKEL: The current. It's against us.

HERMAN: Get a move on. There's more coming.

FINKEL: I can't find the entrance. Where's the pipe?

HERMAN: Dive Finkel, dive, I'll follow your flashlight. Dive.

FINKEL: But you'll be left ...

HERMAN: Dive!

(FINKEL dives, splashing)
Three left. You'll know that Herman and Finkel were here.

The greatest alligator hunters in New York City.
BLAM BLAM
(dives, splashing)

Scene 23

HERMAN: I made it out finally. By the light of Finkel's flashlight. A tough current.

They gave us more shells next time. After two months there were hardly any left. Three months and there was no trace of them. We'd wiped them out.

Whatta you do when you're a New York City alligator hunter and there aren't any alligators in New York?

I went on welfare.

SECRETARY: Will you fill out this form please?

HERMAN: But I already filled out two.

SECRETARY: Yes, I see. An alligator hunter. Oh come off it. How long you been in New York?

HERMAN: All my life.

SECRETARY: An alligator hunter in New York. Sure mister.

HERMAN: No, really.

SECRETARY: Get off it. Look, I don't have all day. The Animal Pound's got a job going, something about catching Gorillas, ha ha ha ha—they must mean monkeys, bothering around the Empire State Building. You want it?

HERMAN: You got to be kidding.

The End

Spiridon

A TRAGIC FARCE
IN TWO ACTS

by

Gregório Eustáquio de Matos Barbosa

Translated from the Portuguese by
Richard L. Epstein

Translator's Introduction

Spiridon is the great work of a playwright about whom we know almost nothing.

Gregório Eustáquio de Matos Barbosa, or Barbozinho as he was called, flourished at the end of the 1600s in Salvador da Bahia, Brazil. Salvador da Bahia in the late 1600s was the sugar capital of Brazil, indeed of the world. Much wealth accumulated there, but culturally the city was a backwater, looking to France for inspiration and standards. How extraordinary, then, that a playwright of world caliber should appear there, and almost as quickly be forgotten. Nothing of Barbozinho's writing has survived other than *Spiridon* and a slim book of verse *Borboletas* (*Butterflies*). Whether his play was ever produced, what reception it might have received, the extent of his fame, all this is lost. We can only surmise that he had some recognition, for *Spiridon* was published in a handsome edition in 1689, one that included stage directions suggesting that the play was performed.

From the text of *Spiridon* we can deduce that Barbozinho knew French and must have had the chance to either read or see a wide variety of the drama of his time. Though he surely would have read Molière, his writing seems to owe more to English and Italian sources. The structure of *Spiridon* is that of a revenge tragedy, a form popular in English drama. But the revenge tragedy goes awry in the style of commedia dell'arte: the costumes, mistaken identities, confusions, songs, and slapstick are all in the Italian tradition. The way in which Barbozinho turns tragedy into comedy in a search for a character's identity is an extraordinary departure from any drama at that time.

A bright flame, a brilliant star across the tropical sky of Bahia, and then forgotten. Yet *Spiridon* still lives.

A note on the text and translation

The text is translated from a copy dated 1689, printed by the brothers João e Ricardo da Costa Marques, Rua Sant'Ana do Agreste, Salvador da Bahia, Brazil. I discovered the work quite by chance amongst some logic texts in the library of the Universidade Federal de Paraíba, in João Pessoa, Brazil in 1991 when I was a visiting professor there. Funds for cataloguing and library conservation are almost nonexistent in Brazil, especially in the poorer Northeast. The book was in poor condition, and the librarian seemed remarkably unconcerned about its preservation, other than to require that it be used only in the library, where there was no copy machine. I have attempted to locate other copies or versions of the play, but actors and directors and librarians I spoke with in Brazil were not familiar with it.

I made a longhand copy of the text in João Pessoa, and, with the help of a colleague of mine, Walter Carnielli in Campinas, São Paulo, Brazil, I made a fairly literal translation. My goal above all has been to turn that rough translation into a script that could be used on stage, one that could convey the power and pace of the original. The rhythms of Portuguese and the ease of rhyming in that language are simply not available in English. I therefore chose to present the work in the form of free verse, trying to achieve some of the rhythmic intensity of the speeches in the meters of American English.

Barbozinho's stage directions are surprisingly extensive for a play of that period. I have added only a few where confusion might arise in English that is not present in the original.

In order to make the context of the play clearer, I have used the American term 'Halloween' in several places, rather than the more literal translation 'All Souls Day.'

Finally, I should like to dedicate this translation to my drama teacher.

> To Nancy Hansen, my teacher:
> imagination, kindness, skills.
>
> "We don't conceal our weaknesses.
> The tragedy is: we conceal our strengths."

Dramatis Personae

SPIRIDON	
PAPOUCHE	*male servant to Spiridon*
PAPILLON	*ex-lover of Spiridon*
BOURDON	*lover of Papillon*
CESTODA	*male hired killer*
GLOW	*female hired killer*
SKEETER	*male*
FAUFILLER	*female*
FALEN	*male*
CICADA	*female*
COOK	*female servant to Spiridon*
SCRUB	*female servant to Skeeter*
BARKEEP	

FAUFILLER, FALEN, CICADA } *guests at Spiridon's party*

Note on the characters

Most of the characters bear French names, and the verse is based on use of the French pronunciation. Portuguese names I have translated into colloquial English.

The characters have the attributes of the creatures whose names they bear:

Papillon - butterfly

Bourdon - drone bee

Cestoda - beetle (pronounced: Ches-tóh-dah)

Glow - glow-worm

Skeeter - mosquito

Faufiller - firefly

Falen - moth (preferably pronounced: Faylen)

Cicada - grasshopper (pronounced: Sée-kah-dah)

Spiridon

ACT I

Spiridon.   One year, seven months, three days,
   One year, seven months, three days.

Since that empty and essential Papillon ran off.
Left, gone, a cold and empty bed still mocks my every night.
She is gone, gone, and I did not follow to thrust and fight
With her foolish love. No! I will not honor his inaneness so.
He does not know, they only toy with some emotions
They solemnly call love. Not even infatuation, but
A silly empty crying after need that they have minded into
Love. My only wish is that they gag and strangle on their
Weft of sighs.

Like a spider's web, where the empty parts describe the pattern.

That I did not rise and slay them, that I did not strike them in
   their sighs,
But only in my sad and lonely wanderings said yes, oh yes,
Do take her, for she never was all mine. No she never
Loved as I had dared, and never wove her web as mine,
Covering all the recesses of her mind. No, I wished them
Well, I, I in my madness even then, for I had seen that
I was but the fly of her desire, the tiny struggling insect
Of her romance, caught and panting in the web that I had wove.
She was no more to me than me myself, just goddess that I
Filled with all my hopes, and said I cannot do you well,
I know you little, my statue of my hopes, so find your little joy.

For little it surely is. Her weak and simple mind can
Know no love as mine. So go, I said. And never knew
I loved her all along. Aye, loved her as only loss can love.
Loved her as the stars in the black and blue chill night now
Fill my bed, where only emptiness and the sometimes moon
   will lie.

But I was fool, oh I was fool. So low, so sad, so tied at mouth
   I only said begone.
And now cry out this one year, seven months, three days.

Even then I did not wholly wish him well. Somewhere within
A cry welled up, and after seven days endured, we met,
Not by chance, and tried to fight, I tried to maim, but
Barely could I lift my arm to shout a strike. Too caught up
    in this
Web of my own making, too like one fly cursing another
And not the Spider that circles slowly for his prey.

Now, now I have shaken off this sickness, this vile smell of my
    own stench
That suffocated all those days. Now I must have her back,
Or more, I must have myself back, and only that with her.
But can I wish to have this used and simple woman to myself?
After all those nights, after days and black cockcrows,
Daylight breaking, still awake, with my vision of her humped with
That dolt. The contours of my love all filled with his unloving
    beastliness.
And now to caress those same and lovely milkwhite arms?
To couple where there always will be
Three? The temple and the two lost travelers.
Oh, I'd always felt a pity for his doltish mind, no fool
But dumb, a buzzing drone that seeks my queen —
Until I saw him coupling, yes, saw him mount my goddess in
    my mind,
How they defiled that poor house. My mind, my mind.
    I have no joy.
Till they are both just martyrs for my love and mind,
I must, I must clean this dread and dusty house where
    my thoughts kneel
Subservient to their love. But how? How?

One year, seven months, three days.

This is the first stage of madness.

One year, seven months — but wait, that's it.
What day's tomorrow?

Papouche, Papouche!

Papouche.   Yes master Spiridon, what is your wish?

Spiridon.   Is my mind deceiving me or is tomorrow Halloween?

Papouche. It is. But I'm surprised you would think of it.
It's a holiday, and you've not smiled on them since
You . . . lost your smile some time ago.

Spiridon. Quite some while ago. Yes. But Halloween.
Perhaps this would be a proper time to recommence my
laughing self.
What do you say?

Papouche. Oh I'd be very glad. Ever since, well, I will not say,
You've been so glum, so low at mouth, eaten so little that
I joy for any sign that you have shaken off your
melancholy chains.
Is there anything that I can do, oh say. For I would
See you laughing, rolling with yourself once more.
Shall we play and celebrate this Halloween?

Spiridon. Yes, perhaps we shall, just that, play some merry pranks.
Papouche, a ball, we'll have a ball. Yes, Papouche,
We'll celebrate this all soul's day with reveling here.
I am ready for my entry to the world. One soul shall rise.
And Papouche, rise not from a pumpkin, eh?
Papouche, some surprises we shall have, eh?

Papouche. We shall, we shall. Surprises for the guests.

Spiridon. And for ourselves. Who shall we invite, Papouche, tell me,
who?

Papouche. Why I hardly know.

Spiridon. Shall we invite my Papillon? Why do you start? And her
Fixed lover Bourdon. Shall we?

Papouche. I cannot tell if you are jesting.

Spiridon. And neither shall they. Come, it is time to make amends.
We shall share our wine with them, let the past slip by.
I am greathearted my Papouche, you do not doubt?

Papouche. I hardly can, your kindness has been great to me.

Spiridon. Well, they shall come. Now listen, you know my wishes
All my ways, so plan the food, the drink, and supervise
the cook.

Go, run, we must hurry, for it shall be tonight.
Yes, tonight, a ball, in costume here. Run, go tell the cook
What we will need and hurry back. By then I'll have a list of
Names that you will stir today to see that they will come.
A ball, Papouche, a ball!

Papouche. I fly!

(*Papouche exits*)

Spiridon. Where I shall weave them in my weft while spirits
    fly tonight.

Oh, that I could forget. But I cannot. We are men,
Not beasts. Two bulls, two bucks in forest fight,
Perhaps to death — one wins, the other sulks away.
One male, one female, a couple fought for now secured.
And the weaker, the buck that slinks away, to find another
Doe or wander in the forest eating grass and pine,
Does he forget? How can he remember? He eats, he sleeps,
He licks his wounds, he fights again. But men!
We fight and lick our wounds until they will not heal.
We lick them with such awful zeal they fester and
    turn black.
We cannot forget, for time's no comfort to the mind
    that knows
The plotting of
Revenge. We count the days.
And now I shall destroy them as the sun destroys the night,
    with
Brilliance overwhelming to their dull and empty heads.
Tonight they die, but first — they know.

This is the second stage of madness.

A list, a list. Here, this list will do. Some years ago
I had a party — we have not changed so much.

(*Enter Papouche*)

Papouche, all is well?

Papouche. As you commanded, here am I again. What shall I do?

Spiridon. Go, rouse these people. Tell them I would have them come

                    To a ball fantastic as the night is long. As jolly and
                    Terrific as this Halloween demands. And tell them all
                    A costume they must wear. No one shall enter here
                        unmasked.
                    Go, tempt them each that they must come. And give, here,
                    This special note to *them*, that *they* will not refuse.
                    Too many days were we good friends for him not to
                        wish us
                    Close again. My silence will have healed it for him.
                    He doesn't think so deep.

                    Go and do it well, for if you do reward will wait.

Papouche. Reward or no, I go, for you. To see such joy and life
                        in you
                    Again, for this I go, I go.

                    (*Exits*)

Spiridon. And I, I go to find a costume for this night, a special
                    Dress to suit the time. And to find a man to help me with
                    My plans. My good Papouche is too much my good friend.
                    I would not have him mired in the mud in which these
                        lovers squirm.
                    I shall find another,
                    A beetle that they shall follow in the night,
                    A glow-worm to lead them to the crevasse of my heart.
                    Oh they are caught and twisting now.

                    (*Spiridon exits*)
                    (*Enter Papouche*)

Papouche. Here, this is it. Yes, this house is right. I still recall our
                        visits here.
                    But this Skeeter, there's little cheer in him!
                    Hello? Hello!
                    He'll buzz all night on money and on men.
                    Hello!

Scrub: (*Within*) Who's there?

Papouche. It's I, Papouche, come with a message from my
                        master Spiridon.

156   Spiridon

Scrub.   (*Within*) Coming, coming.
         (*Enters*)
         Well, what is it? Run, run, run all day long. Scrubbing floors,
         Mending, cooking. Well, speak up young man. My master's
         Work enough for an army of ants. I can't stand here all day long.
         Do this, do that. What do you want?

Papouche. To give your master this. Stop, tell him it's important that
           He come. It's a party for my master.
           Go, run, tell him now. I'll wait.
           (*Scrub exits*)
           Some master this. He'd sting her if he'd dare.
           I'm lucky to be with gentle Spiridon. His kindness pays me well.
           (*Scrub enters*)
           What did he say?

Scrub.   What do you expect him to say? He's coming, and now
          No thanks to you I'll not finish by supper. Go, he
          Says, and buy a costume, or rather rent one, and cheaply, too.
          No finish to my work.

Papouche. My thanks, and if that's not enough, take this to mend your day.
           (*Scrub exits*)
           That's over! Now to a task that I enjoy, to Faufiller's. What a sweet
           Light she casts on all. This door here. With her
           Luminescence she'd brighten Spiridon for sure.
           Perhaps a mistress here to soften his unease.
           (*Knocks at door*)

Faufiller. Yes.

Papouche.   It's I, Papouche, do you recall me? For my master Spiridon.

Faufiller. Of course, how could I forget? I'm delighted you've come.
            Is Spiridon his hearty self again? Good news from there?

Papouche. Indeed, there's to be a ball tonight. For Halloween. With costumes. We'll be very pleased if you can come, Please say yes.

Faufiller. A ball! How wonderful. Then he's
Jolly again. Oh Spiridon, we'll be glad for your smiles and cheer once more.
And Spiridon's parties! Tell him how pleased I am he's thought of me.

Papouche. With all my heart. How glad we'll be to see this night.

Faufiller. When Spiridon resumes his hearty ways. I'm delighted.

Papouche. I go.

(*Faufiller exits*)

Now to the next.

(*Papouche exits*)
(*Enter Spiridon — a bar*)

Spiridon. The Yellow Wasp. It's foul enough in here to find a worm to turn my plans.
You, where is this insect you said will fly my path?

Barkeep. There, nestled with the woman in his drink.

Spiridon. And best not drunk.
(*Spiridon takes Cestoda by the shoulder from behind*)
You, they call you Cestoda?

Cestoda. (*surprised, afraid*) What!? Glow?

Glow. (*slinking off*) Just going for a beer.

Spiridon. I need your hand. Can we talk?

Glow. It looks all right to me.

Cestoda. Don't ever come to me from behind. That's dangerous.

Spiridon. Can we talk with her here?

Cestoda. Glow's as good as I.

Glow. Is there some grub for us in your needs?

Spiridon. Perhaps. But how do I know that you can earn my love?
Tell me, Cestoda, have you ever killed a man?

Cestoda. A man. Hah! Why in this very tavern last week . . .

Glow. Shut up you fool. We make our living with our knives.
Would you want a watch? That's silver there.

Cestoda. I can turn a corpse for you.

Spiridon. It seems . . .

Glow. . . . or a gold one? It won't take long to . . .

Spiridon. It seems that you have all the traits I want, but . . .

Cestoda. But what?

Spiridon. Can I ask?

Glow. Does he look like he'd flinch?

Spiridon. Could you, could you kill — no, worse — maim, then kill
A woman?

Glow. I'll do your job. Your wife, eh? Old? Ugly?
You want to start a new life. We'll blot her out.

Spiridon. She is not old nor ugly. She is young, as spring,
And lovely as the hills all covered with new grass,
Careless as the trees in the wind . . .

Cestoda. Do you want her dead
Or a portrait painted? We're yours if you've the cash.

Glow. Your design's not hard. But maim?

Spiridon. I want no memory of beauty there.
Here's the plan. I'll have a party at my house, tonight.
A ball in mask for Halloween. You'll come in costume,
  like the rest.
And keep your mouths closed — every word you utter will
  unmask you there.
Here, here's some cash. There's more, much more later.
You must go to get some costumes, at this address.
He'll fit you there, then hurry to my house.
We've snares to set for this harlot and her lover.

Cestoda. Hey.

Spiridon. Not you. My harlot and her lover. They'll regret this day,
And then . . . What's wrong?

Glow. Give it to me. He can't read so well.

Cestoda. A lie, damned woman, a lie. We'll do as you've described, Mr. . . . ,
Mr. . . .

Spiridon. Spiridon, it's written there — Spiridon, as in spider.

Cestoda. You've set us on your ways.

(*All exit. Enter Papouche.*)

Papouche. Everyone's so delighted. There's pleasure in Spiridon's errands —
A welcome at every door. They'll come: Cicada and Falen, too.
Cicada will clear the stale air, for sure.
Her chipper ways. And with her voice — perhaps she'll sing for us.
And Falen, too. Hahaha. Pure excitement.
It was all I could do to tell him when and where.
"A party, a party." He's blinded with the glamour of it all.
A young fool's still the best. And Spiridon will laugh
To see him fly to every woman like a moth about a flame.
Oh, he'll be singed, but it's what he wants.
If only it weren't for this. No choice now. He hopes that
There'll be kindness all around. It's for the best.
If only Papillon won't answer. How can I see her
And not cry remembering Spiridon.
May we all be friends.

(*Knocks.*)

Bourdon. (*Within*) Yes, who is it?

Papouche. Papouche.

(*Bourdon enters.*)

Bourdon. Papouche!? How welcome you are, with news from Spiridon? Papillon!

Papouche. No, please. I've a message here.
            He wants to see you both tonight, at a masquerade at home.
            For Halloween, dancing, a ball, in costume, and please,
            Oh please say yes, that you will come. He's been
               distraught,
            You know. You once were friends. Bourdon, help him to
               recover
            His happy ways.

Bourdon. (*reading*) Yes, tonight at nine o'clock. What
               Papouche?
            At last, a reconciliation. Ever since that night I've
            Missed his friendship. It's time he forgot what's past.
            I, well, yes I'll speak to him tonight. Tell him we'll come.
            In costume, of course. And tell him we're pleased.

Papouche. I shall.

            (*Bourdon exits*)

            And hope that there's relief for Spiridon in this.
            He'll meet Papillon with less dread now. They never
               meant him harm.
            The time, the time, cook will scold for sure.

            (*Papouche exits. Enter first Bourdon, then Papillon*)

Bourdon. Papillon. Papillon.

Papillon. Bourdon, dear, what is it?

Bourdon. Look, an invitation from Spiridon.

Papillon. From Spiridon?

Bourdon. To a ball for Halloween. Tonight. He must be tranquil now.

Papillon. At last. Bourdon, this tension's been too strong.
               How he cried, and
            Cried, and pestered us at every hour. Yet why? Tell me,
               Bourdon, why?
            When I lived with him he didn't want me. Not me.

Bourdon. Or so it seemed.

Papillon. Why should he be so upset? Why is the world
            So complicated by his ways?

Bourdon.	I wish I knew. We never thought to wound him.
	He often said that you would drag him down, a weight.
	How many suppers we three had, when he'd ask me so
	    he'd not be
	Bored. There was cheer in our talk. Still, he wasn't happy
	    with you then.

Papillon.	Bored, bored he was. Always circling in his mind. I remember that night well—it seems so long ago — When he told me that he'd nothing he could offer me, Nothing but his sadness, with that dying face of his, and that Nothing I could do would cheer him up, but that his melancholy Had to spin itself out. So I let him spin away in his corner, As he wished. What could I do? Then you were there.

Bourdon.	I understand he may have been upset. But surprised?
	Surprised? As if he'd lived all his life in the dark.
	He surely must have meant for us to be together. What else
	Did he suppose would come of it? Time and time again
	    he'd say
	He didn't know if you were right for him. What was
	    that strange
	Way he said? "Dancing different planes."
	That's it.

Papillon.	Yet you and I were just the same. We understood, not like his darkness.
Bourdon.	And so we're here. Come Papillon.
Papillon.	Still I try to figure out his change. He was so jolly when we first met. Alive. Yet even when you went to tell him the next day, Like a friend, he wasn't screaming as he later did.
Bourdon.	No. He took it as one would inevitable, the loss. He seemed to weave around a hole I'd made for him, Creating a pattern as I watched. Eerie, that's what I thought. He almost seemed relieved.
Papillon.	Bourdon, why must some people be always hurt? He can't want it so?

	Why even when I went to ask him for some trinket, some sign he wasn't
	Mad, on my birthday, you remember, he surely must have been resigned by then!
	And why shouldn't he be happy for us? Why?
	He only yelled and made me feel just awful, as he screamed those names at me.
	He loved us both once, why not together?
Bourdon.	He's strange to me, but still I like him, I wish him good. For his kindness, and the friendship we once had.
Papillon.	And now we'll have again. We'll go, and I'll bring some Happiness to him too. Now all is well.
Bourdon.	Indeed, we should bring him a gift to mark this day, To show we care, that we understand how much it means.
Papillon.	A gift!
Bourdon.	What shall it be?
Papillon.	I know: some slippers that he likes. His were always worn; he'd never remember to buy them for himself, I know just the kind.
Bourdon.	A lovely gift.
Papillon.	I'll find a pair. No one else would know but me.
Bourdon.	While I go to get some costumes.
Papillon.	I'm so excited now. A party. We'll dance and he will Laugh again.

(*Bourdon and Papillon exit. Enter Cook and Papouche*)

Cook.	OK Papouche, OK. It is good news, I agree. I'll be glad to see a happy face on him — enough of those Mournful sighs. But it's work for me. You, you go off to the Fine folk's homes, and they invite you in and you chat, and I have work to do.
Papouche.	Oh, work, work. Here, I'll help you.

Cook.   Papouche, you're a fine fellow. I swear you'd help someone if they'd
Just sigh. Well, I won't say no. Come on, then.
Reach me that pot.

Papouche.   This one? But what can I do when you bend over?

Cook.   Help me and stop fooling around. There's plenty of food, for dozens like you said.

Papouche.   Dozens? Ten, maybe twelve. Cook?

Cook.   Ten or twelve?! You said dozens.

Papouche.   A baker's dozen, I bet that's it. There's nothing for it now. We'll just be eating well for longer than we thought.

Cook.   For weeks I'd say. All that food. Oh Lord.

Papouche.   Cook my love, don't worry. This party will set everything at ease.
Besides, you've little to complain about. I've cleaned the house
From top to bottom, and still have the silver left to do.
You women don't know how lucky you are.

Cook.   Oh we don't, eh? I'd like to see you stand in front of this fire all day.
You'd wilt, hahaha, that's it, you'd wilt.

Papouche.   Come on, nothing of the sort.

Cook.   Just like that night, when was it, after Christmas, when you drank too much. Like a flower on a stem. Oh Papouche.

Papouche.   You don't have to remind me.

Cook.   Come back here then. It only took some tender care to bring your flower back to life. Silly Papouche.

Papouche.   Enough of that. As I said, I've lots of work to do.
Wilted flower, hah, we'll see tonight.

Cook.   Oh we will? Get out now. Go on. You just said you had your work.
And I can smell the roast is nearly done.

Papouche. A mouthful?

Cook. Here, before you go.

(They exit. Enter Spiridon)

Spiridon. Now I have firmly tacked the corners of my web about this ball:
The outer edges all are wove and now I spin, I spin,
Down to the center where my lover and my love shall wait
To be devoured by this spider's lust that they provoke.
Not seeing they are trapped still will they squirm and
Wriggle as my two insects carry off their better parts.

Papouche! Where are those deathly actors to trace out my designs?
Papouche! My costume. Is all in readiness?
The time approaches. And now, and now.

(Papouche enters dressed in spider costume)

Papouche. Everything's going as you wish, and cook and I . . .

Spiridon. What's this? What? What costume have you there?

Papouche. Why just the one you ordered.

Spiridon. I'm to be the spider.
What's this? My costume then is what?

Papouche. It's here.

Spiridon. Devil take the one who made our costumes. He's switched our
Sizes thoroughly. A clown!
Devil take the one, this mask is bad.

Papouche. It's too late to change.

Spiridon. It is indeed.
I shall have to be content. That fits you well at least.
Here, help me with this top. I'll leave the mask till later.
Now good Papouche is all in order?
This costume vexes me.
The wines and roast, the decorations as I've said?
You know my will in all these things.

Papouche. All nearly ready; we've little time and if you've no need of me, I'm off.

Spiridon. Go, go, but wait. No one has rung?

Papouche. None.

Spiridon. Two old friends will be here shortly, ones you've never met. I'm expecting them. Show them up. And don't be alarmed. Their manners may not seem as mine, but I have known them long.
Old friends must be remembered still, though we have changed.

Papouche. I'll know them then since they'll be the ones I don't know yet. I go.

(*Papouche exits*)

Spiridon. Oh time you suffocate me still.
Race on, race on, let this night begin and lift the darkness from my soul.

(*Spiridon exits. Enter Skeeter in costume, no mask.*)

Skeeter. And see that all's locked up. If you value your job you won't fall asleep.
Worry, worry. First I have to rent a costume, then leave my goods
With a drudge like that.
And no friends of yours in there tonight. You hear!?
He charged too much, but what could I expect.
Hastily mended, this color's too bright.
What, what's this? A tear? What's he take me for?
All this worry for a ball. Were it any but Spiridon's I'd never go.
And there's money. If this marks the end of his
Weakness, good, for I've markets for his wealth.
And Faufiller. She's sure to come.
I've waited long enough alone: silence won't prevail.
If my good looks and form won't tempt her, this bauble will.
Not like Papillon. Silly woman, spending his all on her.
Beauty yes, but

	I'll not be stuck to one like that. Faufiller, ahhh,
	Now she could warm my bed. Her brilliance is tempered with a mind I like.
	She'll know sense when I show her this.
	I'll hover round until the time is ripe.

(*Enter Faufiller in costume, no mask.*)

Faufiller. Don't wait up. Just leave the candle there. I'll not be back till dawn.

Skeeter. Faufiller . . .

Faufiller. Oh, Skeeter, you startled me.

Skeeter. I beg your pardon. You're going to Spiridon's?

Faufiller. Why yes, to his dance. What a lovely night.

Skeeter. Yes. I'll accompany you then. You'll take my arm?

Faufiller. More gently Skeeter, there.

(*They start to exit. Enter Falen in costume, no mask.*)

Falen. Hurrah for a dance on all soul's eve
Where a love will come to me.
Oh moonlight leads to madness,
And madness leads . . . to glee.

Faufiller. Oh look, Falen.

Skeeter. Let's hope he's not going to Spiridon's.

Falen. Skeeter. And Faufiller. Ahh, look at that golden harvest moon.
What a spell it casts, though pale beside your lovely glow. There's love tonight.

Faufiller. Good evening Falen.
I can see you're going to Spiridon's. Will you join us?

Skeeter. Aaaagh.

Falen. Hurrah, to Spiridon's. And his fantastic parties.
There'll be madness in this night.

Skeeter. In any case a lot of noise. Join us if you must, but stop the poetry.

	And with this silly costume. We'll need someone to point out the moon to us.
Falen.	You can laugh if you wish Skeeter. But tonight there's a real spell of love.
Falen.	You're both amusing. Come, one arm for you, and one for you. To Spiridon's.

(*They exit. Enter Papillon and Bourdon in costume. No masks.*)

Bourdon.	Hmmm. This costume's tighter than I thought. Does it suit me? I must be getting fat.
Papillon.	Bourdon, kiss me. How I hope this all goes well. You have the slippers?
Bourdon.	Yes, yes, don't worry. It'll all be fine. We're friends again. How splendid you look. Come now, smile. There'd be no party if he still felt bad.
Papillon.	You're right of course. Why else would he have this celebration? We're friends now. He'll laugh and be jolly again, knowing we are too.

(*Enter Cicada in costume, no mask.*)

Bourdon.	Look, Cicada. Oh Cicada, Cicada.
Cicada.	Bourdon? Papillon? Vous, vous, excuse me, but your costumes. Vous, . . .
Bourdon.	Yes, to Spiridon's. It's like old times; we're friends again.
Cicada.	Ahhh, bon. I am so happy. For Spiridon will I chanter tonight. A little song, non? To celebrate we are all happy again. We shall make him so gay.
Papillon.	Singing at Spiridon's. It will be good.
Cicada.	I am for you, too, also so happy. Monsieur Bourdon, you will escort me, non?
Bourdon.	Of course.

168 Spiridon

(*They exit. Enter Cestoda and Glow in costume, no masks*)

Cestoda. Look at this, look! I tell you this costume's wrong.
Here, I can't reach my knife. Glow!? How can I turn a Corpse like this?

Glow. Don't be ridiculous. Here, you've got that part on backward.
For what he's parting with tonight I'd feel sillier than you look.
And tonight we're at a ball. Cestoda, finally, a ball.
And the pay besides!

Cestoda. Money. For me there's something in his turn,
Some thread of speech that leads me on.
Something more than money guides my hand tonight.

Glow. You may like his perverse taste, but it's his cash I want.
Go ahead, knock.

(*He knocks. Papouche answers the door*)

Cestoda. To see Spiridon. He knows who we are.

Papouche. Good. We were expecting you.
I'll tell him that you're here.

(*Papouche exits*)

Cestoda. Who was he?

Glow. A servant, some part of him. Go on.

(*Exit Cestoda and Glow.*)

(*Enter Spiridon in clown costume, no mask, followed by Cestoda and Glow.*)

Spiridon. It's you then? Are you ready? Your costume's aren't too bad.
Papouche, leave us now. Cook's to be helped and the guests will soon be here.
Come to me later; we talk on subjects far from you.

(*Papouche exits.*)

You're ready then to wind destruction like a web?

Cestoda.	What?
Spiridon.	To squash the butterfly and drone, That butterfly, Papillon, the simple woman that I loved.
Cestoda.	Yes, but . . .
Spiridon.	And do it well? I want some beauty in their death, An outline of suffering against my mind.
Cestoda.	Yes, but . . .
Spiridon.	I've traced this web within my mind. We'll net them as they dance. Give me your hands. Your hands!
Cestoda.	That's it! This costume, here, I'm stuck, no there. Look, I can barely reach around. My breath is nearly Sucked out — this costume's not for me. I'm warning you it won't work unless . . .
Glow.	Will you shut up? Let him explain his plans. We'll do it your way.
Spiridon.	It can't be helped. The one who makes our costumes isn't apt. Let's turn to forms of death.
Cestoda.	Then tell us what you want.
Spiridon.	You're to be among the guests — I'll say that you're old friends, From growing up. Don't talk more than you must, you'll attract Suspicion like dung attracts a fly. Then you'll lure Papillon, that name unmans me still, And Bourdon to the paths outside, while I entertain the guests. The garden, there, in back will do.
Glow.	Where?
Cestoda.	I don't understand.
Spiridon.	In the back, you'll see when you go down. You'll lead them to a spot of darkness, and then, and then . . .
Cestoda.	That I know. Murder's a thing I understand.

Spiridon. You'll call me when they're squirming,
When you're squeezing out their cruel lives;
Trapped in darkness as I am now.

Glow. Wait a minute, do you want regular murder, or some perversions, huh?
The perversions will cost you extra.

(*Bell rings*)

Spiridon. There's no time now, the guests are here. Go on down.
I'll trace the scheme in detail later.
Use your imagination. Your lives are soaked in murder,
I only know from darkness.

(*Bell rings. Cestoda and Glow exit. Bell rings.*)

I come, I come, down to meet them all.
And when dawn breaks new visions will be mine:
Two insects mounted mating on a pin, formaldehyde and all.

(*Bell rings*)

Down, down I go, and they with me.

This is the third stage of madness.

END ACT I

ACT II

(All characters are now in costume and mask, except for Cook who will have neither.)

(Enter Faufiller, Skeeter, Falen, and Papouche)

Faufiller. How lovely. Isn't it splendid that Spiridon's in humor now?

(Papouche takes her wrap.)

Thank you Papouche. Listen to the music.

Falen. To bewitch us. And the odors, the air perfumed, the candles. Magic, magic. Only a man who's loved contrives a ball like this.

Skeeter. Hmmm, love. There's too much noise to hear the music well.

(Enter Spiridon with his clown's mask — bulbous red nose, etc.)

Faufiller. Spiridon. We're all so glad you've asked us to this ball.

Spiridon. Faufiller. You look radiant. Welcome.
And Falen, Skeeter, you're both welcome to this special dance.
We've been apart too long.

(Papouche comes in and out at various times with wine, taking wraps, etc.)

Falen. Yes, Spiridon, we know . . .

Skeeter. This wine's not bad. Your taste — still the same.

Falen. Wine? Why the very air will make us drunk tonight.

Spiridon. And Falen, how are you? In love or falling still?

Falen. You laugh, but your plans betray that you've a heart. Romance, romance is the mood, and I'm for it.

Spiridon. A heart? We all have one. When that's used up?
Falen, Faufiller, will you do me the honor to begin the dance?
I'll join you when the other guests arrive.

Faufiller. Delighted.

Falen.   We fly.

          (Faufiller and Falen exit.)

Spiridon.   Skeeter, is it business makes you grimace so? You said the wine was good.

Skeeter.   That cowsick boy and her. Business, yes, the market's on my mind.

          (Bell rings.)

Spiridon.   Papouche, see who's there.
Business, and the world makes you richer still.

Skeeter.   Me? Never. I have to sting them for every drop.
There's a little piece I'd like to speak to you about.
Your help . . .

          (Enter Papouche.)

Papouche.   Spiridon, Bourdon and Papillon are here. Shall I bring them in?

Spiridon.   Bourdon and Pap . . . Pap . . . excuse me Skeeter.

Skeeter.   I'll go in. Think of your proper business now.

          (Skeeter exits.)

Spiridon.   Must I meet them now? Papouche, my mask.
Papouche, they're here?
My mask, this costume's right?

Papouche.   As it should be. They're anxious, too.
I told them that tonight we're friends again. How glad they are.

Spiridon.   You told them? And Papillon was glad?
My mask! I must meet them now.

          (Papouche exits.)

          Pulse be still. I must compose myself.
Remember heart, I am the spider now.
Slowly lead them to the center of my . . .
Pulse, be still.

          (Enter Papouche, Bourdon, and Papillon.)

Papouche.   Together again. My master and you two.

(*Spiridon motions Papouche off. Papouche exits.*)

Spiridon. Bourdon. Papillon.

Bourdon. Spiridon, we're glad to see you. You know as well as I that . . .

Spiridon. Welcome.

Papillon. Spiridon, we're friends again, at last. How silly your anger was then.

Spiridon. Silly.

Bourdon. No bad will now. No harm intended.

Spiridon. We're joined at last.

Papillon. You know we've missed you awfully. And I worried about you.
We hoped that time would heal . . .

Spiridon. Friends. No need to talk of before.
Tonight ends that.
I'm glad you're here.

Bourdon. See, I told you it was all past.

Papillon. Bourdon was right, you aren't upset. I'm so happy then.
Shall we dance?

Spiridon. Go on within while I greet the other guests.
And I'll warn you, two friends of mine, you might not recognize them,
They're here tonight. They'll seek you out.

Bourdon. Good, we'll look for them. We'll have a long chat later.

(*Bourdon and Papillon exit.*)

Spiridon. So with this mask it's not so hard. Perhaps I will enjoy this night
If my tears will let me see.
Papillon! You tear my heart with your cruel innocence.
Cruelty! Innocence! Shredding of my heart.
My soul is damned for you.

(*Spiridon exits. Enter Cestoda, Glow and others, variously, to dance.*)

Cestoda.	You're sure you know which ones they are?
Glow.	Yes, them. The two together. Now you'll dance with her, and bring her close to this corner Where I'll draw her off.
Cestoda.	Me? Dance? Are you kidding? Who said this?
Glow.	Don't you ever listen? Just now he explained. I suppose you were playing with your costume.
Cestoda.	Shut up about my costume, will you? I feel like a fool in it. But did he really say I was supposed to dance with her? Glow, me?
Glow.	Yes, you. You said yes just two seconds ago. You can do it can't you?
Cestoda.	But Glow, me?
Glow.	Just like at the Yellow Wasp, only not so rough. You dance her over here, and . . .
Cestoda.	But listen to that music. I wasn't expecting that. Look Glow, let's just change the plans and . . .
Glow.	We can't now, he's promised us twice as much to follow his pattern. Get on out there will you?

(*Cestoda approaches Papillon while Glow conceals herself.*)

Cestoda.	You dancing?
Papillon.	What?
Cestoda.	I said, you dancing?
Papillon.	Bourdon, who is he?
Bourdon.	I don't know with that mask. It must be that friend of Spiridon.
Cestoda.	Well?
Bourdon.	Go on, you can't very well refuse. Spiridon might be hurt.

Papillon. Shall we?

(*Cestoda and Papillon dance, he a clumsy bar room style, attracting attention. He does a fast step and splits his trousers.*)

Cestoda. Thanks a lot. Yeah. I got to go.

Papillon. Thank you very much.

(*Small laughter generally from others who return to dancing.*)

Cestoda. Glow. Psst. Glow.

Glow. What happened? I was waiting for you.

Cestoda. It doesn't matter. Do you have a needle and thread?

Glow. What do you mean it doesn't matter? What happened?

Cestoda. You didn't see anything?

Glow. No, I've been waiting here.

Cestoda. Good. Nothing happened. She didn't want to dance. It wasn't a good idea.

Glow. Oh great. What'll we do now?

Cestoda. First we get a needle and thread.

Glow. Are you still going on about your costume? Oh.

(*Exit Cestoda and Glow.*)

Cook. Tell me how they looked.

Papouche. Papillon's still beautiful. And Bourdon a little fatter.

Cook. And the others, all the ladies in their gowns?
Papouche, with the sights and perfumes in the hall will you still think of me?
Down here, sweating with these cakes and meats . . .

Papouche. It's only you I think about. And your sweetmeats.

Cook. Papouche. Here, let me wipe my hands.
No, not with that silly mask on. There.

176   Spiridon

	(*They kiss.*) Now hurry up with this. I've work to do.
Papouche.	And they wait for me upstairs. (*They exit in opposite directions.*)
Cestoda.	We'll do it my way now, OK?
Glow.	OK, but how?
Cestoda.	I've got it all figured out. This time it's your turn. Play up to that Bourdon, yeah you know how. Don't give me any stares, you do it for a living don't you?
Glow.	Why you lowly crawling pimp, if that's what you think. I've never made my living on my back, though this wouldn't be The first time you suggested that I should. If you ever . . .
Cestoda.	So you're not a whore. I only meant you're smart enough to be one. Now . . .
Glow.	Oh.
Cestoda.	Now you play up to him, make him follow you into the garden. You have your knife?
Glow.	Here.
Cestoda.	Only if he gets rough. We'll do this as Spiridon laid out. I'll be out there hidden.
Glow.	Good.
Cestoda.	I'll wait in here till I see the sign, then I'll go first.
Glow.	Got you.
	(*Cestoda and Glow separate. Glow approaches Bourdon, mimes a seductive approach, unsuccessful, cries, etc. Finally Bourdon escorts her off. In the meantime the following dialogue is going on.*)
Cicada.	Allo. You are the friend of Monsieur Spiridon who we are to be looking for, yes? Non?

Cestoda.	What? Yes, yes. Spiridon's friend.
Cicada.	You are enjoying the party? Spiridon he is very happy, and generous, non? Quel musique.
Cestoda.	Yeah, the music's ok.
Cicada.	You are playing hide and seek, yes? It is a game?
Cestoda.	That's right, a game.
Cicada.	Ah bon, I too will hide?
Cestoda.	A private game.

(*Cestoda gets the sign from Glow and rushes off.*)

Cicada.	Très bizarre.

(*Cicada returns to others at the dance. Bourdon and Glow are exiting to the garden.*)

Bourdon.	There, there, don't cry. There's no reason to be upset.
Glow.	You don't know. The scars I have.

(*They exit offstage. From the garden area offstage come the sounds of splashing water, much commotion, cries of help, and general confusion. Enter Glow, Cestoda, and Bourdon. Cestoda is dripping wet.*
Papouche enters later attracted by the commotion.)

Glow.	Are you all right? (*To Bourdon*) Stop slapping him will you?
Cestoda.	Aaagh.
Bourdon.	That was a nasty dive you took. Here, hold your arms up like this.
Cestoda.	Get him off me will you?
Glow.	Listen, thanks a lot. I better take care of him.
Bourdon.	I hope you're not hurt. There's nothing I can do?
Cestoda.	Nothing.
Bourdon.	You're sure?

Cestoda. Nothing!

(*Bourdon exits.*)

Papouche. I'll fetch Spiridon.

(*Papouche exits.*)

Glow. What happened?

Cestoda. What do you mean, what happened? I fell in didn't I? No one told me there was a pool out there. Damn.

Glow. What was wrong, you couldn't look where you were going?

Cestoda. Once more like that and Spiridon'll get three for the price of two.

(*Enter Spiridon and Papouche.*)

Spiridon. Enough Papouche, I'll take care of it now.

(*Papouche exits.*)

What happened?

Cestoda. Oh no, you too? Can't you see?

Spiridon. You didn't try to drown him?

Cestoda. No! There's a pool out there. Why didn't you tell me there was a pool out there?

Spiridon. You mean to say you just fell in?

Cestoda. Just?

Spiridon. Why didn't you look where you were going?

Cestoda. Why didn't you tell me there was a pool out there?

Glow. Calm down will you, they're watching us.

Spiridon. So nothing's happened yet. Nothing.

Cestoda. OK, then you talk to him.

Glow. Nothing. Look, if you want it done your way give us a plan we can do.

Cestoda.	But first I've got to get out of this costume. It's starting to shrink.
Spiridon.	You're right, you can't stay like that. Where can . . . Wait, Papouche.

(*Enter Papouche*)

Papouche.	Yes.
Spiridon.	Go up to the attic and see if you can find a costume in those trunks. One that will fit my friend.

(*They start to go; Spiridon grabs Cestoda.*)

And don't foul it up this time. (*To Glow*) You, you stay.

(*Papouche and Cestoda exit.*)

Listen, I thought you knew your trade.
Don't explain. Just listen.
Go on up after them and see he gets fitted.
Then bring Bourdon to my study, the first door there.
I'll place Cestoda within. Send him to me. I'll explain it
   so even he can understand.

(*Glow exits.*)

These two are more like moths that crash into the walls
   than the
Wasps I thought I had. They'll serve me though.
This scheme is foolproof. Subtlety's too slippery now.
And I am anxious.
Be done. Be done.

(*Exit Spiridon. Enter Faufiller and Falen.*)

Falen.	Faufiller, each moment with you is filled with the soft glow Your charm spreads out.
Faufiller.	Falen, you're very sweet, but I'd rather not dance. Let's sit.
Falen.	Some wine then.
Faufiller.	Thank you. Falen, look at all the lovely women Spiridon's invited.

	With all this beauty you mustn't spend your time with me. And I should say hello to other friends.
Falen.	What women? When the music, the moon, the air all speak of you. Faufiller, my heart . . .
Faufiller.	Now hush, Falen, please. I now what you're going to say. Don't look so sad. I've no thoughts of romance tonight, I'm having too much fun. And so should you.
Falen.	But Faufiller . . .
Faufiller.	Leave romance for another night, some beautiful girl who loves your Poetry. There'll be many.
Falen.	I wish I could meet one.
	(*Enter Skeeter to them.*)
Skeeter.	You again? More poetry? Won't your lines sell here? Eh? No? Faufiller, will you take some air with me?
Faufiller.	Skeeter, now don't be cruel.
Falen.	I know when I'm not wanted.
Skeeter.	Don't feel bad. Your poetry's harmless. Why don't you try it out on someone else? Like Cicada. She's your type.
Faufiller.	Yes, Falen, she's very sweet. She sings, and would like your way. Try.
Falen.	I'll see you later. Don't forget what I've said.
Faufiller.	Go on, she hasn't any beau. We'll talk some other time.
	(*Falen exits.*)
Skeeter.	At last. Finally I'm alone with you.
Faufiller.	Why Skeeter, if I'd known I'd have danced with you before.
Skeeter.	No matter. Faufiller, we've lived next door for how long now?

Faufiller. I can't guess. Years and years. But I hardly know you.

(*Enter Glow.*)

Glow. Have you seen that big guy? You know, Bour. . ., Bour. . .

Skeeter. What, what? Bourdon? Yes, over that way.

Glow. Thanks.

(*Exit Glow.*)

Skeeter. Yet I've watched you. You've a light that attracts me.
I'm older, no one close to me. No one to leave everything I own.
It's time we knew each other better.
Take this, a token of my interest in you.

(*Skeeter gives Faufiller a brilliant brooch or ring.*)

Faufiller. Skeeter! I'd have never thought . . .
This is dazzling. But it's so sudden.

(*Commotion from the direction of Glow.*)

Skeeter. What's that?
Yes, my interest in you. You must be my wife.
I'm in earnest. Don't refuse me.

Faufiller. What works men's minds to set them on us so?
I'll think Skeeter. Your gift delights me though.
Shall we dance?

Skeeter. Dance? In that crowd? Take my arm, we'll walk about.

(*Exit Skeeter and Faufiller.
Enter Spiridon and Cestoda separately.*)

Spiridon. Ah, Papouche, is everyone satisfied?

Cestoda. I'm not Papouche.

Spiridon. What? Cestoda, where did you get that costume? You didn't . . .

Cestoda. It's the only one your man could find.

Spiridon. But this is impossible. It's the same as Papouche. And he?

Cestoda. He's still got the same. Look, I'm not so happy with it myself,
But at least it fits.

Spiridon. Papouche, you — and I was supposed to be the spider.
At least it's dry. Now listen carefully.
Glow is to lead Bourdon to my study. You'll be there, wait for me.
There, the first door. There. Leave off the lights.

Cestoda. Good. This sounds better. I'd rather be fast.

Spiridon. Then your heart's like mine. Place yourself.

(*Cestoda goes.*)

And I will nudge my Papillon to this same dark hole.

(*Exit Spiridon. Enter Cook and Papouche.*)

Papouche. So he fell in. We made him up in one of Spiridon's old suits.
He's rough — I never knew Spiridon had such friends.

Cook. Still it's good he won't deny them. You ought to remember that.
He does right by his friends.
Spiridon's all kindness in the end.

Papouche. You're right cook. It's his heart we work for.
Talking about work, is that platter ready? Come on, they're waiting.

Cook. Here. And don't take more than that.
If you get drunk then I can't serve.

(*Exit Cook and Papouche. Enter others.*)

Cicada. So, I will sing for you a song. You are wishing it, non?

All. Yes, yes. Do go on. Splendid. Marvelous.

Cicada. Bon. Then I begin.

(*Sings*)
Like a child running for a butterfly
We chase our fancy;

	Half crouched we spring for the sunlight On a thin curved wing of hope we fly.
All.	Bravo. Lovely. Very beautiful.
Cicada.	It is good to sing, yes? So happy.
Spiridon.	Papillon, I'm not much for dancing. Let's talk awhile. Come into my study, and tell me of the happy life you lead.
Papillon.	Happier now by far that we can talk.
Spiridon.	I lead her to the darkness of myself.
	(*Others have returned to the dance. Spiridon and Papillon enter the study. Sounds of thumping and cries from within. Papillon runs out, followed by Spiridon staggering after.*)
Spiridon.	You fool, you fool. It's me. Lay off. It's me.
Papillon.	Spiridon, are you all right?
Spiridon.	Just a game, Papillon, a game, a friend surprised me. Halloween and . . . ohhhhh.
Papillon.	You're hurt. I'll fetch Papouche, Some water for your head.
Spiridon.	No! I'm all right, come in . . . (*Staggers*) oh oh oh. Yes fetch Papouche. My head.
	(*Exit Papillon. Enter Cestoda from the study.*)
	You blind dimwitted worm. (*Strikes him.*)
Cestoda.	Do that one more time and your life is mine. It's dark in there.
Spiridon.	And now you've missed your chance. That was Papillon, the one that you're to kill. Now you know what she looks like. Yes? Ohh.
Cestoda.	It's your fault. You said that Bourdon would come first and then . . .
Spiridon.	It doesn't matter. Can you handle that knife?
Cestoda.	I tell you yes, if I've the chance.

Spiridon. Then Bourdon enters next. Knock him out — do what you will.
Just stay in there and use it when you see your prey.

Cestoda. I'll be ready. Just one clear chance is all I need. This is more trouble than it's worth.

Spiridon. Go in, go in, you'll be paid well.

(*Nurses head, turns, Cestoda enters study, Papouche then enters*)

Go in, I said, go in.

Papouche. But where?

Spiridon. In there like I said.

Papouche. Here? But you never said . . .

Spiridon. Don't argue.

(*Papouche enters study. Sounds of struggle from within.*)

Spiridon. What?! Stop. Stop.

(*He drags out Papouche.*)

Are you all right? Papouche? Papouche?
Answer me, are you still alive?

Cestoda. Did I do right or did I do right? I told you if you gave me a chance . . .
Bring him back in here where I can finish him off.

Spiridon. Papouche. (*Papouche moans*) My better half still lives.
Back in there and hope you haven't killed my best friend.

Cestoda. Look, am I supposed to kill him or not?

Spiridon. Not him! Bourdon. You're like a fly that lights on any blood it smells.
The next will be right I promise. And then Papillon.
Get in there.

(*Cestoda enters study.*)

Papouche, speak to me.

Papouche.   Oh my head. What, oh cook you were right
That wine creeps up on you. Ohhhhh.

Spiridon.   Can you stand?

Papouche.   Stand? Oh master Spiridon, forgive me,
I've drunk too much and now . . .

Spiridon.   There, there, it's all right as long as you haven't hurt yourself.
You hit your head when you fell. Take my arm, that's it.
We'll go downstairs where cook can help you.
Hold on. Easy now.

(*They exit. Enter Falen and Cicada.*)

Falen.   And then old Skeeter stretched his nose like this.

Cicada.   Hahaha. Falen, you are making me to laugh. You are very funny.

Falen.   But serious, too.

Cicada.   Oui, serious. Your poetry, she is serious, non?

Falen.   As serious as love.

Cicada.   When you talk like so I am getting the chills.
Have care what you say Monsieur Falen.

Falen.   Why? Can it be that you sense what I am feeling?

Cicada.   Why is it that you would know?

Falen.   Because, Cicada, your voice, your gaiety, your beauty
All excite me so. What joy we could have.

Cicada.   It is so? If I could but be believing you.

Falen.   Believe me. I've fallen in love before, but never to
A woman who stirs my heart like you. When you sang, Cicada,
It stirred all the poetry of my soul.

Cicada.   And your poetry is me too stirring. But Falen, many women, non?
With your pretty face, yes.

Falen.	No. None like you. Cicada, as the moon is breaking through the clouds, So my love shows itself to you. Slowly, gently . . .
Cicada.	And mon coeur to you, also, is showing itself. You are comprehending, non?
Falen.	With all my heart. Together we'll share the songs and poetry of life.
Cicada.	Oui, we two. We dance now — you will be holding me close, yes?
Falen.	Yes. Spiridon, love's woven in your music now.

(*They dance off. Enter Bourdon and Glow.*)

Glow.	Bourdon, I need someone strong. My husband's a miserable roach. He beats me too. Someone strong like you, who's loving.
Bourdon.	Me? But . . .
Glow.	Bourdon, come in here and let me tell you more.

(*They enter the study. Thrashing and screaming.*)

Glow.	Beat me will you? Take that!

(*She chases Cestoda out, beating him.*)

Insect, worm, insect, worm.

Cestoda.	A mistake, ow, a mistake, ow, ow. I'm sorry.
Bourdon.	Her husband's jealous. He'd never understand.

(*Bourdon exits*)

Cestoda.	Ow, ow. Enough. Enough. I said enough.
Glow.	You whimpering worm, it's me Glow.
Cestoda.	I know that now.
Glow.	What's wrong, you're too stupid to turn on the light?
Cestoda.	He said to leave it off, and the next one would be, would be . . . Papillon, that's right. How could I know it was you?
Glow.	You fool. Bourdon was one step back. If you'd waited we'd be half done by now.

Cestoda.	So it's my fault? You could have made some sign.
Glow.	O.K., O.K. That Spiridon doesn't know what he wants. We'll kill them before he stretches out another plan: Here, or there, with both hands, or just one. We'll show them death as it's meant to be.
Cestoda.	My hand itches for their life. Those two are laughing at us. To kill the rich, well let's get on. I love the murder I'm set on now.

(*They exit. Enter Spiridon.*)

Spiridon.	This little vial of poison's death enough for one. Now it must do. Those stinking worms I've brought are Mindless. They'll never serve me right. I'll pour this bane for Papillon. It's enough That she must die, she, that vessel where I poured my love. Now take your poison back, the vile dripping of my days.

(*Exits.*)
(*Enter others in turn.*)

Falen.	Cicada, my love, we'll fly.
Cicada.	Oui, tonight. We are happy, non?
Falen.	To find you here, it all seems so unreal. This evening, The dance — love's fated in the magic here.
Cicada.	Oui, and I am finding you, too.
Skeeter.	Then you'll say yes.
Faufiller.	I'll not promise anything.
Falen.	Skeeter, Faufiller, aren't you glad? What a magic night. With Cicada I've found . . .
Skeeter.	Someone to accost with your poetry.
Faufiller.	Then I'm glad.
Bourdon.	It's certainly gone well.
Papillon.	His cloudy passions are gone at last. It must have been a Stage, some term he had to live.

Faufiller.	Bourdon, Papillon, All's well? Then Spiridon must be happier, too.
Papillon.	Yes, reconciled.
Bourdon.	We're friends once more.
	(*Enter Spiridon with a tray of drinks.*)
Spiridon.	A toast, a toast, here, everyone, a toast.
	(*They take glasses.*)
	Wait, wait, that's right. There, for you Papillon.
Papillon.	Thank you Spiridon.
Falen.	A toast to moonlight, dances, love, and . . .
Bourdon.	Friendship.
Papillon.	Yes, friendship.
Spiridon.	And visions born tonight. Drink up, drink up.
All.	Here, here. (*They drink.*)
Spiridon.	Excuse me, excuse me please.
	(*Runs off choking and gasping.*)
Cicada.	Such emotion.
Papillon.	He's so sensitive.
Faufiller.	How lucky we are to have a friend like Spiridon.
Bourdon.	Yes, lucky indeed.
Skeeter.	It's late. We must go. Where's Papouche? Falen, find our wraps.
	(*Falen goes.*)
Cicada.	We are all going?
Papillon.	On this happy note.
Faufiller.	Yes, happy. We must go, it's nearly dawn.
Skeeter.	You'll accompany me. My drudge had better be awake.

(Falen returns with wraps.)

Faufiller. Will you join us Falen, Cicada?

Falen. We'll go by ourselves. Cicada.

Cicada. Oui, we two.

Skeeter. Bourdon, you're not going yet?

Bourdon. We'll wait to say goodbye to Spiridon.

(They are putting on their wraps, beginning to depart during the next speech.)

Spiridon. Wait! Are they leaving? Wait you can't go yet.
Ugh, that poison's foul. I'll never lose that taste.
At least my wits were up enough to spit it out.
Wait! Hold up, the night's still young.
Oh, the puking and the wine, my system's all awry.
And my head where that idiot struck me.
Wait. The web is all for nought, the strands are broken,
I can barely see the pattern now. Wait.

(Throughout what follows Spiridon is stupefied.)

Bourdon. Spiridon, too much to drink?

Spiridon. They're leaving?

Falen. A wondrous eve. Spiridon this Halloween's
The essence of romance.

Cicada. Merci from me, too, and au revoir Spiridon

Skeeter. We'll speak on business soon.

Faufiller. Thank you Spiridon. Good night.

(All exit except Papillon, Bourdon, and Spiridon.)

Papillon. We only stayed to say goodbye. And Bourdon,
   the slippers.

(Cestoda now swings out on a rope from offstage. His intent is clear: to swing by Papillon and Bourdon, striking them with a knife as he goes. But he misses and goes out of control, smashing into the wall on the other

side of the stage. He screams out, swings back, and is now terrifiedly out of control. He will swing back and forth at appropriate places till the end, eventually slowing down, occasionally crying out, while Glow yells: Hold on, hold on.)

Spiridon. Oh no. What? An old friend, someone from days you didn't know.

Bourdon. Odd. I have the package here.

Papillon. These are for you, to remember this night. How we're all friends.

Spiridon. Slippers?

Papillon. It's good we can be friends again. Your moods are gone now? May I?

(*Kisses him on the cheek, Cestoda swings by.*)

Is your friend all right?

Spiridon. Slippers. You knew I needed slippers?
You'd touch me still so close?

Papillon. Of course, I'd never forget something like that.
Your feet get so sticky.

Bourdon. Goodnight. Come to our home now.

Papillon. Goodnight.

(*She kisses him again, then exits with Bourdon.*)

Spiridon. AAAaaaaaaaagggggggghhhhhh. She still would touch me near my heart.
Slippers, knife, it's all the same. Papillon, your
Cruel innocence is worse than all the blows the world can
Strike.
Aaaggggh. Visions. No love.
Visions through this aching dawn!
Dawn! What light can force the shadows from my soul?
Papouche! Papouche!

(*Cestoda and Papouche enter from opposite sides,*

both very wobbly, uncertain, barely able to stand. Still both costumed and masked as spiders.)

Papouche? Papouche? Cestoda?

(*Neither responds, both out of it.*)

This is the, this is the . . . first stage of madness.

THE END

Essays in logic and philosophy

Three Questions about Logic

Logic, whether formal or informal, is meant as a guide to reasoning. From that perspective arise three questions about the foundations of logic as the art of reasoning well: On what basis should we choose which logic to employ? On what basis do we decide between the descriptive and prescriptive aspects of a logic? What heuristics do we use in evaluating the strength of an argument?

Question 1

In *Propositional Logics* I asked the question:

> If logic is the right way to reason, why are there so many logics?

The answer I proposed, based on readings of the writings of originators of many logics, is that which logic you use depends on what you are paying attention to in your reasoning. To use classical logic we allow ourselves to attend to only truth-value and form. For all other logics we attend to (at least) one additional aspect of propositions: how we come to know a proposition is true (intuitionistic logic), subject matter of propositions (relatedness logic), the ways that reference is achieved or intended by a proposition (dependence logics), the likelihood of our being right in our ascription of truth to a proposition (many-valued logics), and so on.

In that book I did not discuss nor have I ever seriously raised the following question.

> *On what basis do we choose which logic we do or should employ?*

I only noted that differences in our reasoning could be ascribed to differences in what we pay attention to in our reasoning, and that those differences could be factored into a structural analysis of reasoning in a regular way.

This is a crucial question. However, no study of logic or logical systems is likely to bring us an answer. We need to examine the uses to which we put logic, for the basis of our choice of a logic is one way we factor goals into our reasoning.

Question 2

More generally, I have understood logic, whether formal or informal, as giving models *of* reasoning that become models *for* reasoning. That is, observations about reasoning are initially descriptive but become prescriptive rules. I have tried to make clear the bases on which certain rules are established, for example the truth-tables in classical propositional logic or the definition of truth in a predicate logic. I have examined many examples as tests of the aptness of the models, showing how problems in analyzing examples lead to modifications or extensions of the theory.[1] But I have not resolved the most important question about logic as models of reasoning:[2]

> *On what basis do we make decisions about throwing out or modifying some rules that aren't descriptive or keeping them and saying that they are nonetheless prescriptive?*

The closest I have come to a general answer is the following.

The basis for models of reasoning is that we make assumptions that guide us in creating a logic, and the results of the logic applied to examples must be in accord with those assumptions. For example, to establish predicate logic we assume that the world is made up of things, and propositions about the world are to be analyzed as being about things. In *Predicate Logic* I show that it is difficult if not impossible to formulate coherent assumptions about language and the world that could be taken to underlie Aristotelian logic, which constitutes a criticism of that logic.[3]

Some assumptions that guide the creation of a logic are metaphysical, some are not. They are all guided by particular interests in the world, which point us to what we feel we should pay attention to in the world. Thus, an answer to this question is connected to an answer to the first question.

Question 3

I have investigated rules for reasoning with arguments, conditionals, cause and effect, explanations, and reasoning in mathematics.[4] There are many subjective elements in the evaluation of all those ways of reasoning.

One particular subjective notion that is crucial to all reasoning is the strength of an inference. A *strong inference* is one in which it is possible but very unlikely for the premises to be true and conclusion false.

Attempts to substitute an objective criterion in terms of probabilities have not been successful.[5] Nor can we eliminate using strong arguments by relying solely on valid inferences as the basis for good reasoning.

The notion of the strength of an inference is highly dependent on what knowledge we take as assumed, and our general background, and interest in the subject matter of the claims involved. Content matters in evaluating whether an inference is good, as can be seen in hundreds of examples in *Critical Thinking*. When others outside the United States teach from that text they find that many examples must be changed, for what is obvious to most students in the U.S. leading to a clear judgment that an argument is strong or weak would leave a Korean or Brazilian student at a loss to determine the strength of the argument.

Though subjective, the analysis of the strength of an inference often, indeed in practice almost always, can be made intersubjective: after enough background information is exchanged, reasoners who originally differed will come to the same analysis.

But I have not previously considered the following question:

What heuristics do we use, what rules do we or can we employ in evaluating whether an argument is strong?

Such heuristics are crucial to reasoning but are not, on the face of it, part of the rules of reasoning. They have to come before we employ inferences. They are part of the background, the human aspect of reasoning that can be examined but cannot, on pain of infinite regress, be formalized and made part of the rules of reasoning.

This question is where psychology, biology, evolution, even ethics meet logic.

These are three questions about the foundations of logic. They cannot be resolved, indeed, they cannot even be understood if we take logic as a gift of the gods, immutable, removed from human interests and concerns. But they are at the heart of logic as the art of reasoning well.

Added July 2022
After a discussion with Eduardo Ribeiro and Juan Francisco Rizzo, it now seems to me that the third question is loaded. The right response to it is: What makes you think there are any heuristics or principles that we do, or can, or should use in evaluating the strength of an argument?

In *Critical Thinking* I propose some very general guidelines: *The Guide to Repairing Arguments* and *Unrepairable Arguments*. The latter is extended by the discussion of fallacies in that book.

These are guidelines. In hundreds of examples I show that the application of them always requires judgment. There are exceptions to the guides, and any principle more specific would be limited to just the one or two cases from which it is formulated.

Evaluating arguments, not just for strength but also for the plausibility of premises is a skill. It cannot be taught as any collection of rules or guides. Only by working through hundreds of examples and exercises in that book can one become somewhat proficient. Even then, new examples will challenge.

This is like what Chad Hansen has taught me from studying his *A Daoist Theory of Chinese Thought*. There is skill that can be exhibited and used but not verbalized, as the story of the cook by Zhuangzi shows: the teaching, the learning via guidelines or rules is shucked off when the cook becomes capable. The difference from argument analysis is that cutting up a carcass does not involve reflection or discussion, while dissecting an argument does. Indeed, discussion and reflection are necessary to arrive at an intersubjective analysis.

Why do we look for principles in logic? For formal logic the answer is because we hope to make explicit how our metaphysical assumptions and grammar influence what we consider to be tautologies and valid inferences. For informal logic, for all the work of analyzing and evaluating arguments, explanations, causal claims, prescriptive claims, indeed even mathematical arguments, there is no comparable motive. We develop our skills with the help of a master.

Compare how reasoning in the law proceeds. General principles are offered in the form of laws. But using those principles in making judgments is a skill that must be learned over years. Common law requires judges to formulate principles governing cases in which the formal laws are not definitive. But those are seen as only guidelines that can be set aside by invoking differences in the case in hand from the one for which the principle was made.

Indeed, logic is the art of reasoning well.

NOTES

1. See my *Predicate Logic, An Introduction to Formal Logic, 2nd edition*, *The Internal Structure of Predicates and Names*, and *Time and Space in Formal Logic*. See also my *Reasoning about the World as the Flow of All* for the same issues relative to a different metaphysics on which are based the logics.
2. This question is raised and discussed in "Prescriptive Theories" in my *Prescriptive Reasoning*.

198 Three Questions about Logic

3. See my "The Metaphysical Basis of Logic: Things and Masses" in my *Language and the World*.
4. See my series of books *Essays on Logic as the Art of Reasoning Well*.
5. See "Probabilities" in my *The Fundamentals of Argument Analysis*.

REFERENCES
EPSTEIN, Richard L.
1990 *Propositional Logics (The Semantic Foundations of Logic)*
Kluwer. 2nd edition, Oxford University Press, 1995. Second edition with corrections, Wadsworth, 2000. 3rd edition Advanced Reasoning Forum, 2012.
1994 *Predicate Logic (The Semantic Foundations of Logic)*
Oxford University Press. Reprinted, Wadsworth, 2000. Reprinted by Advanced Reasoning Forum, 2012.
1998 *Critical Thinking*
Wadsworth. Fifth edition with Michael Rooney, Advanced Reasoning Forum, 2
2006 *Classical Mathematical Logic (The Semantic Foundations of Logic)*
Princeton University Press.
2011 *Cause and Effect, Conditionals, Explanations*
Advanced Reasoning Forum.
2012 *Reasoning in Science and Mathematics*
Advanced Reasoning Forum.
2013 *Prescriptive Reasoning*
Advanced Reasoning Forum.
2013 *The Fundamentals of Argument Analysis*
Advanced Reasoning Forum.
2015 *Reasoning and Formal Logic*
Advanced Reasoning Forum.
2016 *The Internal Structure of Predicates and Names*
Advanced Reasoning Forum.
2021 *Language and the World: Essays New and Old*
Advanced Reasoning Forum.
2022 *Time and Space in Formal Logic*
To appear, Advanced Reasoning Forum.
2023 *Reasoning about the World as the Flow of All*
To appear, Advanced Reasoning Forum.

Is There a Problem with Formal Semantics for Natural Languages?

Abstract
A close examination of a paper by Jeffrey Pelletier in which he offers formal semantics for mass nouns and count nouns raises the question of what justification there can be for using the methods of formal logic in the study of meaning in natural languages and what is the study of meaning.

Introduction
I must be confused. People have been working on formal semantics for natural languages for more than fifty years. There are many books and papers on that subject. Yet I cannot figure out what they are doing. Perhaps if I write down what I see as a big problem in formal semantics for natural languages, someone can enlighten me.

A paper by Jeffrey Pelletier, "Lexical Nouns Are Both +MASS and +COUNT, But They Are Neither +MASS Nor +COUNT", raises the issues clearly, most particularly what justification there can be for using the methods of predicate logic to study meaning in natural languages since predicate logic is prescriptive and is based on a metaphysics that is not compatible with much of how we talk and understand.*

If I understand Pelletier's paper correctly, his basic idea is that a noun such as "chocolate" or "lamb" is neither a mass noun nor a count noun until it is used in some phrase, and even then it might depend on context. If we say "a chocolate" then we recognize that

---

* The problem of forcing meaning to be understood through the metaphysics of predicate logic is exemplified but not confined to Pelletier's work on mass nouns. Terrence Parsons work in *Events in the Semantics of English* shows that such a focus can lead to eliminating verbs in the analysis of English, as I show in "Events in the Metaphysics of Predicate Logic".

For those who are familiar with formal semantics for natural languages it should be clear that the issues raised here apply generally. For those who are new to the area, this paper can serve to guide their reading to look for how a theory deals with mass terms and process words, the analysis of which is outside the scope of modern formal logic, as I explain in "The Metaphysical Basis of Logic: Masses and Things".

it's a count noun; if we say "some chocolate" we're treating it as a mass noun. When we say "some lamb" we're treating it as a mass noun; when we say "a lamb" we're treating it as a count noun. Both "chocolate" and "lamb" by themselves are neither mass nor count. His denial of a semantic distinction between mass nouns and count nouns depends, it seems to me, on the following:

> ... are there really any words that are atomless—whose referent has no smallest parts? Doesn't *water*, for example, have smallest parts: H_2O molecules, perhaps? Certainly *coffee* and *blood* have smallest parts,* as do other mixtures. A standard defense of the divisiveness condition in the face of those facts is to distinguish between 'empirical facts' and 'facts of language'. It is an empirical fact that water has smallest parts, it is said, but English does not recognize this in its semantics: the word *water* presupposes infinite divisibility.

 It is not clear that this is true, but if it is, the viewpoint suggests interesting questions about the notion of semantics. If *water* is divisive [atomless] but water isn't, then water can't be the semantic value of *water* (can it?). In turn this suggests a notion of semantics that is divorced from 'the world', and so semantics would not be a theory of the relation between language and what a speaker's mental understanding is, since pretty much everyone nowadays *believes* that water has smallest parts. Thus, the mental construct that in some way corresponds to the word *water* can't be the meaning of *water* either. This illustrates a kind of tension within natural language metaphysics.

* footnote: At least, there are volumes that contain coffee, and there are subvolumes of such a volume which are so small that they do not contain coffee. And so some sort of 'continuity principle' suggests that there is a cut-off line or interval that yields smallest parts of coffee.

 Pelletier says that "pretty much everyone believes that water has smallest parts". Where is the study that shows that? Some people, perhaps a lot, have been told that water has smallest parts, some kind of small thing, perhaps they know the word "molecule" or even "H_2O". But that doesn't mean they believe it. People have been told that a table is almost entirely empty space with atoms and electrons zinging around, but they know very well that a table is solid. They've been told that water has smallest parts, that's "science", the talk of scientists, but that doesn't mean they believe it, though they may parrot it if asked. And that's just the people who've heard the phrase "H_2O molecule".

Perhaps it is a standard response to say water has smallest parts yet our language doesn't recognize that. But it's been known and commented on for a long time that water has no smallest parts. As I explain in my essay "Models and Theories", if water were just collections of H_2O molecules, then no one would ever have drunk water, for what we call "water" is invariably a mixture of H_2O molecules and much else. Even in a laboratory it's not possible to obtain a sample of "pure" water. When we talk of muddy water, of clear water, of sweet water, of salt water, we are clearly not using "water" to refer to a substance that is composed of only H_2O molecules. Our abstraction of the stuff in the world we call "water" has smallest parts. We pay attention to just this one aspect of the stuff we call "water" and investigate that. A scientific theory does not give meaning to words; we do.

In the footnote (*), Pelletier invokes a continuity principle to support his contention that coffee, and by extension other masses, has smallest parts. But that's the the drawing the line fallacy: if you can't make the difference precise, then there's no difference, as I explain in *The Fundamentals of Argument Analysis*. In any case, I think he would be hard put to apply the same to "mud" or "air".

More fundamentally, Pelletier is wrong about the nature of semantics and meaning. Meaning is what we do, as I explain in "Language-Thought-Meaning". Semantics, as we use the term in logic and linguistics, is how we abstract from that. Pelletier has left no room for people to be inconsistent in the way they conceive of their experience and the world. So someone sometimes thinks of water as having no smallest parts, and at other times thinks of it as composed of H_2O molecules. That some people try to force one of those conceptions as the only one in order to have a clear theory is their problem. But that is just what Pelletier is trying to do in this quote that continues the previous one:

> Further problems with the semantic approach to the mass-count distinction come from the fact that there are pairs of words where one is mass and the other is count and yet the

items in the world that they describe—or in the minds of the speakers using the terms—seem to have no obvious difference that would account for this. On the intuitive level, it seems that postulating a *semantic* difference should have some reflection in the items of reality that the terms designate (or in the mental life of speakers using the terms). But this is just not true. There seems to be nothing in the *referent* (or speaker belief/intentions) of the following mass vs. count terms that would explain how they should be distinguished, as they intuitively are . . .

    a. Concrete terms
- (i) baklava vs. brownies
- (ii) spaghetti vs. noodles
- (iii) garlic vs. onions
- (iv) rice vs. beans

    b. Abstract terms
- (i) success vs. failures
- (ii) knowledge vs. beliefs
- (iii) flu vs. colds

So at one time people figured that garlic should be assimilated to the category of masses. Why? Who knows? Conjecture: we crush garlic and the crushed garlic is like a mass, just as "lamb" for the meat is a mass. For spaghetti, we talk of spaghetti noodles, but spaghetti itself has tomato sauce etc. and viewed like that it does seem to be a mass. One noodle of spaghetti is not spaghetti, nor are two noodles of spaghetti (the drawing the line fallacy looms). The odd one is rice vs. beans, but that's not so strange: we can count beans if we want, while grains of rice are so small it's almost impossible to count them; Brazilians disagree and use the mass term "feijão" for what we call "beans".

    The problem is the conception of semantics Pelletier has, not the conception of mass vs. count. Language works by analogy, and we may have a fairly strong conception of mass that we use for the archetypal examples: mud, water, gold, . . . and which we extend to other "stuff" like that because it fits our views, or did at some long-ago time when the language was becoming settled, so that we talk of rice and garlic as masses. No problem with that unless you think that language categories must map perfectly onto the world.

I think we have a robust conception of mass vs. individual thing. We should be able to devise an experiment to test that. But I cannot see how, since we would have to use language to do the experiment and our language already has the "solution" fixed into it.

The confusion I have with Pelletier's conception of semantics really shows up when he gives his own theory of mass nouns.

> We discussed the example of *beer*, in whose extension we find not only the semi-lattice of beer, but also individual servings of beer, standardized types of individual servings of beer, kinds of beer, and perhaps other types of values as well. In the present proposal, all these will be part of the semantic value of the lexical item *beer*.
>
> In more general terminology, the proposal for lexical semantic value is this. Given a]— Abst] lexical noun N, its (extensional) semantic value, $\mu(N)$, would be (something like):
>
> $$\mu(N) = \{N^o \cup N^m \cup N^s \cup N^{ss} \cup N^k \cup \ldots\}$$
>
> that is, the union of all things of which it is true. (N^o represents the objects that are N; N^m is the material that N is true of; N^m are the standard servings of N; N^{ss} are the standard sizes of servings of N; N^k are the kinds of N; etc.)

What does Pelletier think he is giving a theory of? How people actually use the language? That doesn't seem likely. I have no idea at all how to fill in the dots. For water, what are the "standard servings", and what is the "material" that N is true of? I thought that material was water. If that's not it, then he's assuming that water is H_2O which is the only way you can get the material to be things. It may be that if pressed someone could fill in some of these collections of "things", though hardly all, but there is no reason to think they would do it consistently from one day to the next.

And how would Pelletier proceed with the mass nouns "running" and "justice"? Pelletier's "standardized servings" seems to be just an appeal to classifier words that we use with mass terms: "a cup of water", "a bottle of beer", "a pond of water". Would a "standardized serving" of justice be "an instance of justice"?

Pelletier is trying to reduce all mass-talk to thing-talk. Doing so he is taking one part of our language—thing-talk—and trying to make it serve for all. I suspect that his motive is to be able to use the tools of set theory and predicate logic in his formal semantics, for that is what the "formal" requires. But predicate logic supposes only that we can conceive of the world as made up at least in part of individual things and that the reasoning in which we're interested is about individual things and their relations, as I explain in *Predicate Logic*. Pelletier needs much more: the world is made up entirely of things and all "truths" are about things and their relations. That's a very strong metaphysical assumption, which modern physicists reject.

Pelletier's theory has to be seen as an abstraction. But an abstraction to what end? When we do something like this in logic it's to the end of finding out what inferences are valid relative to certain assumptions, especially metaphysical assumptions since those influence the syntactic assumptions. But what is the goal of such an abstraction here? To help us . . . what? If this is descriptive linguistics, Pelletier should be able to quote a big study here that shows that people do conceive of nouns in this way. If it's "regularizing" or "making precise" a part of how we use language, I again have to ask: why do that? For logic the answer is obvious: to help us reason better, to draw out inferential relations in our web of meaning, relative to the metaphysical and linguistic assumptions we make in establishing our logic. But here I can find no clear motive. It seems to me that Pelletier is using the tools and approach of formal logic for no clear end.

But perhaps I have missed the point and someone will enlighten me why formal semantics for natural languages is not just nonsense.

REFERENCES

EPSTEIN, Richard L.
   1994 *Predicate Logic*
           Oxford University Press. Reprinted by Advanced Reasoning Forum, 2012.
   2012 Models and Theories
           In *Reasoning in Science and Mathematics,* pp. 19–51, Advanced Reasoning Forum.
   2013 *The Fundamentals of Argument Analysis*
           Advanced Reasoning Forum.
   2015 Events in the Metaphysics of Predicate Logic
           In Epstein, *Reasoning and Formal Logic*, pp. pp. 131–136 Advanced Reasoning Forum. Reprinted as Appendix 2 of *The Internal Structure of Predicates and Names,* Advanced Reasoning Forum, 2016, pp. 227–230.

2021   *Language and the World: Essays New and Old*
2021A Language-Thought-Meaning
      In EPSTEIN, 2021, pp. 60–85.
2021B The Metaphysical Basis of Logic: Masses and Things
      In EPSTEIN, 2021, pp. 107–116.

PARSONS, Terence
   1990   *Events in the Semantics of English*
        MIT Press.

PELLETIER, Francis Jeffrey
   2012   Lexical Nouns Are Both +MASS and +COUNT, but They Are Neither +MASS nor +COUNT
        Count and Mass across Languages, ed. Diane Massam, Oxford University Press, pp. 9-26.

Mechanical ≠ Computable

Abstract

The notions of computable and mechanical are often taken to be the same, but they are not. A criterion that distinguishes them has consequences for whether a person's behavior could be modeled by a computable procedure.

A mechanical procedure need not be computable

Suppose we construct a machine that can pick up two dice, shake them, roll them out, read the top two faces, and print out the sum of the dots on them. The procedure can be viewed as a function: associate to the number n the nth printout once the machine is started.

This dice-rolling procedure is mechanical: it is effected by a machine.[1] Intuitively, however, it should not be classified as computable. But if so, then some general criteria for a procedure to be computable are needed. A. A. Mal'cev lists five [2]:

a. An algorithm is a process for the successive construction of quantities. It proceeds in discrete time so that at the beginning there is an initial finite system of quantities given and at every succeeding moment the system of quantities is obtained by means of a definite law (program) from the system of quantities at hand at the preceding moment of time (*discreteness of the algorithm*).

b. The system of quantities obtained at some (not the initial) moment of time is uniquely determined by the system of quantities obtained in the preceding moments of time (*determinacy of the algorithm*).

c. The law for obtaining the succeeding system of quantities from the preceding must be simple and local (*elementarity of the steps of the algorithm*).

d. If the method of obtaining the succeeding quantity from any given quantity does not give a result, then it must be pointed out what must be considered to be the result of the algorithm (*direction of the algorithm*).

e. The initial system of quantities can be chosen from some potentially infinite set (*massivity of the algorithm*).

The question about (a) is whether the dice-rolling has a program. But the law is very simple: ignore the previous quantity and roll the dice again, then print out the number of dots on the top face. We can even assume the machine is run by a computer and these instructions are coded into a computer program.

Criteria (c), (d), and (e) are satisfied by the dice-rolling procedure.

The remaining criterion, (b), however, would seem to rule out the procedure as computable: We want to say that the outputs of the dice-rolling machine are not determined. They are random.

But then we have the general question of determinacy. Wouldn't the physicist say that the outputs are determined by the initial state of the machine? That is, after all, the basis of physics, since there is nothing random in the actions of the machine.

It is wrong to invoke determinacy as a criterion for computability: the classification of the dice-rolling procedure as computable shouldn't depend on whether we are determinists. Indeed, what is random, what is predictable is usually explained in terms of computability.

Perhaps the difficulty is that we can obtain only a finite number of outputs no matter how long we run this machine, whereas for a computable procedure we are to have a program that will define a function for all values of *n*. But as noted above, there is a program. And it assigns outputs for numbers as large as we are prepared to wait. The difference between concrete and abstract, hardware and software is not in itself sufficient to differentiate between mechanical and computable.

But isn't the program of the dice-rolling machine connected intimately to *this* machine? No, we could run another similarly built machine with this program. But aren't the *answers*, the outputs we get, dependent on running the program *this* time on *this* machine?

Yes, and that is the basis of the distinction between what is mechanical and what is computable. For a procedure to be computable it must be *duplicable*: barring mechanical failure, we must obtain the same results each time we run the program.[3]

Duplicability and artificial intelligence
Some current efforts in artificial intelligence begin with or are designed to test the hypothesis that a mind/brain can be modeled as a computable procedure in terms of its inputs and outputs.

But the mind/brain procedure fails the criterion of duplicability. Like the dice-rolling machine, it may be mechanical, but it is not computable. The input/output relation is intimately connected to the procedure *this* time on *this* machine (body).

Lack of duplicability is not an accidental feature of the mind/brain. The brain (machine) changes, the inputs change.

But then why do some say that some creatures, say a dog, is nothing more than a machine, in the sense of computable, predictable? Juney will *always* bark at the sound of footsteps outside the front door when she's inside, assuming that her body (machine) is functioning correctly. She will always chase a ball when it's thrown. At least till she died last year.

We claim her behavior (input/output relation) is predictable/computable, that it is duplicable. But it is not her entire behavior, even though a substantial part of it. And duplicability is not in terms of *exactly* the same inputs: the sound of the footfall is always a bit different, the ball can't be said to bounce the same way always. No, we think animal behavior is predictable, duplicable because of equivalences we put on behavior. For "equivalent" inputs Juney will react and give "equivalent" outputs.

For us to argue similarly for humans on any broad scale would require criteria of equivalence on input. What would determine whether two experiences are "identical"? And don't we mean, in any case, "identical for all our purposes"? Wouldn't identity of inputs depend largely on the language and culture of the observer, contrary to what we would want for a procedure to be classifiable as computable?

Nonetheless, for some limited aspects of human behavior we do have clear, well-defined, agreed-upon criteria for identity of inputs and for identity of outputs. For example, adding: the inputs are pairs of numerals, no matter how those are presented, and the outputs single numerals. For chess, the input is the opponent's move, and the output a move, no matter how those are described. In these cases there has been success in devising computable procedures which, though not duplicating any particular human's activity, duplicate the general nature of the activity in such a way that we agree that the computable procedure adequately models the behavior.

In sum, then, conjectures cannot be falsified if experiments cannot be duplicated. The conjecture that the mind/brain is a computable procedure confuses the mechanical with the computable. Duplicability is lacking in the input/output relation of human behavior. We can, however, establish criteria of identity on behavior in certain limited fields of human activity and then hope to model those activities as computable procedures.

NOTES

1. Bertrand Russell, "On the notion of cause", *Proceedings of the Aristotelian Society*, 1912–1913, in *Mysticism and Logic*, 1925, Longman, Green and Co., pp. 180–208:
> A system may be defined as "mechanical" when it has a set of determinants that are purely material, such as positions of certain pieces of matter at certain times.

2. A. A. Mal'cev, *Algorithms and Recursive Functions*, Walters-Noordhof, 1970, pp.18—19.

3. This analysis was first presented in Richard L. Epstein and Walter Carnielli, *Computability: Computable Functions, Logic, and the Foundations of Mathematics*, Wadsworth & Brooks/Cole, 1989.

Intentions

We take "Spot wants to play" to be about Spot and what he wants: a desire. We understand "Flo thinks that coyotes are dogs" to be about Flo and what she is thinking: a thought she has. We take "Suzy believes that Spot will bite Puff" to be about Suzy and what she is believing: a belief she has. It seems natural to us to talk of thoughts, beliefs, and feelings as things

I will present here a different way to understand such sentences that invokes no mental objects, no talk of thoughts, beliefs, feelings, but rather ways of thinking, believing, feeling.[1]

Background: the metaphysics and parsing of our ordinary speech
I start with an assumption that is basic in our ordinary speech.

The world is made up, at least in part, of individual things.[2]

In accord with this, I will limit investigations here to sentences that are or can be construed to be about individual things, excluding an analysis of sentences that involve mass terms and process words.

Relative to this assumption, I make the following definitions.

Proposition   A *proposition* is a written or uttered sentence that is used in such a way that it is true or false, but not both.

Names   A *name* is a word that is meant to pick out a specific individual thing.

Predicates   A *predicate* is any incomplete phrase with specified gaps such that when the gaps are filled with names the phrase becomes a proposition.

A pronoun that is meant to pick out a specific object in context is a name.

---

[1] This project arose in my work in *Time and Space in Formal Logic*. The presentation there is embedded in formal logic analyses of reasoning taking account of time. Here I hope to present the ideas and methods without appealing to formal logic while using examples only in the present tense.

I am grateful to members of the Advanced Reasoning Forum (ARF) who in online discussions helped me understand this topic, and to Arnold Mazotti who helped me clarify a nearly final draft.

[2] This seems natural to English speakers and speakers of European languages. But it is not basic for speakers of many other languages, as you can read in my *Language and the World: Essays New and Old*.

I take propositions and predicates to be linguistic. Those who think that propositions are abstract or mental can take what I call a proposition to be a representative of what they consider to be a proposition. Still, those people have to rely on linguistic representations of their propositions in order to communicate with us, or more to the point, to reason with us. Similarly for predicates.

We can take the following as a simple proposition so long as we are not concerned with its internal structure:

(1) Spot is barking.

When we consider its internal structure as made up of a name and predicate, most logicians and linguists write it the same way. But doing so does not clearly demarcate the predicate from the name. To make that division clear, I'll write (1) as:

(2) (— is barking) (Spot)

In logicians' terminology the condition for this to be true is that the predicate "— is barking" is true of the object named by "Spot".

Consider, too:

Dick is taller than Zoe.

Marking the predicate and names clearly, we have two blanks in the predicate:

(— is taller than —) (Dick, Zoe)

The terms "Dick" and "Zoe" fill the blanks in the predicate "— is taller than —".

Predicate restrictors[3]

If we are not concerned with the internal structure of propositions, we can take the following to be a simple proposition:

(3) Spot is barking loudly.

If, however, we wish to relate (3) to (1), we must consider its internal structure. We have (2), and we need to show the role of "loudly" in (3). That word does not apply directly to Spot, for it makes no sense to say that Spot is loudly. Rather, it is meant to apply to the predicate "— is barking". We can mark that by using a back slash to write "((— is barking) / loudly)". Then we can write (3) as:

---

[3] This analysis of predicate restrictors is developed formally in *The Internal Structure of Predicates and Names*.

(4) ((— is barking) / loudly) (Spot)

The predicate in (4) is "((— is barking) / loudly)". It is simple in that it contains no logical particles (connectives, quantifiers, etc.), though it does have internal structure. In (4) "loudly" *restricts* the predicate "(— is barking)". To evaluate whether (4) is true or false we first consider all those things for which "(— is barking)" is true, then restrict to those which are barking loudly, and then ask whether Spot is one of them. So if (4) is true, so is "(— is barking) (Spot)", and that's correct, for if (3) is true, so is "Spot is barking".

Variable restrictors
Consider:

(5) Spot ran to Dick.

If (5) is true, so is "Spot ran". The phrase "to Dick" is acting as a restrictor. We can view "to (—)" as a variable predicate restrictor that becomes a predicate restrictor when the blank is filled with a name. So we can write (5) as:

((— ran) / to (Dick)) (Spot)

This, too, is a simple proposition: it contains no logical particles. Whether it is true or false does not depend on the logic we adopt.
    Now consider:

(6) Dick threw a ball.

To evaluate (6) we ask first whether Dick threw. That makes sense even though it sounds wrong in English because we demand a direct object for "threw". But we can ask: "What did Dick throw? A ball? A stick? A rock? A dog biscuit? A banana peel?" For each of those as an answer we can say that Dick threw something. And, though it sounds odd, we can say equally that he threw. We are not going to have our metaphysics determined by the grammar of English, as if the difference between a direct object and an indirect object is based on some nature of the world. Some transitive verbs in English are not transitive in other languages and vice versa, while some languages use only a few or no prepositions.[4] So, if (6) is true, so is "Dick threw". That is what we have with predicate restrictors. But there is no mark in (6) that "a ball" is being used as a restrictor, for we do not mark direct objects

---

[4] See *Language and the World*.

in English. So let's take "obj (—)" as a marker for direct objects, a variable restrictor. Then we can rewrite (6), using x to stand for a pronoun "it":

There is some thing x such that:

((— threw) / obj (x)) (Dick) and (— is a ball) (x).

Intentions

Consider:

(7) Flo wants a dog.

Following what we did with (6) it seems we should parse this as:

(8) There is some thing x such that:

((— wants) / obj (x)) (Flo) and (— is a dog) (x)

But this is wrong. For (8) to be true, there has to be at least one specific dog that Flo wants. Yet Flo is wanting to have a dog without her wanting being directed to any one dog: Flo has a disposition, not a mental condition (thought) directed at some object. It is not correct to take "a dog" as a direct object of the verb "wants".

So what is the role of "a dog" in (7)? If (7) is true, then so is "Flo wants". That is, "a dog" is acting as a predicate restrictor. How can we show that? We have the predicate "— is a dog". We can mark that as the restrictor, writing (7) as:

(9) ((— wants) / (— is a dog)) (Flo)

This seems so odd to speakers of English that some explanation that would justify (9) as true if (7) is true seems needed. I can offer one approach, though I want this analysis to be open to others. We could say that Flo has a concept of a dog, where a concept is not a fixed thing, not a mental thing nor an object, as I describe in "Language-Thought-Meaning". That concept gives the way Flo wants; it is part of her disposition. Flo's whole body is involved in her wanting in that way.

Now compare:

(10) Spot wants to play.

If there is no thing that Flo wants in (7), then even more so there is no thing that Spot wants in (10), for there is not even a hint of an object in the grammar.

Suppose that (10) is true and so is:

(11) Dick wants to play.

A colleague said that we can conclude from (10) and (11):

(12) Dick and Spot want the same thing.

This is at best misleading. In (12), "thing" is no more significant than "It" is in "It's raining". Rather, Dick and Spot want in the same way. But that, too, seems wrong, for it makes ways into things. Rather, the infinitive "to play" is being used as a restrictor. We can indicate that:

((— wants) / (to play)) (Spot)

((— wants) / (to play)) (Dick)

If both (10) and (11) are true, we have:

(*) The same predicate "((— wants) / (to play))" is true of both Dick and Spot.

We do not have to invoke some thing that both Dick and Spot want.

Sentences as restrictors

Consider now:

(13) Suzy hopes that Zoe will call.

If this is true, then so is "Suzy hopes". This suggests that "Zoe will call" is acting as a restrictor in (13). We can make that explicit by writing (13) as:

(14) ((— hopes) / (Zoe will call)) (Suzy)

It is sometimes said that using "that" creates an *oblique context* in which, in this example, "Zoe will call" appears. There are debates about whether in such a context, "Zoe will call" is or should be construed as a proposition, with the definition of "proposition" adjusted according to the answer. In (14) "Zoe will call" is viewed not as a proposition but as a restrictor. It is meant to direct us not to a way the world is or could be, but to how Suzy wants, no more a proposition than "to Dick" is in "Spot ran to Dick". This is why I do not include "that" in (14).

Those who say that "Zoe will call" as it appears in (14) is a proposition accept that its truth-value doesn't matter in evaluating (14), as it doesn't for (13). But that's to say that "Zoe will call" is not used in such a way that it is true or false, which means it is not a proposition according to the definition with which we began.

If one still contends that "Zoe will call" is being used as a proposition in (14), what if "Zoe will call" is false? Then we have to say that Suzy is hoping for something false. I can't make sense of that. (If the future tense bothers you, consider "Zoe hopes that Dick washed the dishes"). What we can have as true is:

Suzy hopes Zoe will call and not-(Zoe will call)

(15) ((− hopes) / (Zoe will call)) (Suzy) and not-(Zoe will call)

Actually, if "Zoe will call" is being used as a proposition in (14), we should rewrite (13) as:

Suzy hopes that "Zoe will call" is true.

And here insert a resolution of the liar paradox.[5]

On the notion of proposition we started with, there is no reason to say that "Suzy will call" is a proposition in (14). It is a sentence.[6] And being a sentence, it is meaningful.

But what does it mean to say a sentence is meaningful?

Meaningfulness

The sentence "Zoe will call" is meaningful. I could leave that open to many interpretations, but that is not enough here. I take the notion of meaningful as in my essay "Language-Thought-Meaning". Suzy understands the words. She might have some idea of what contexts would make it true or would make it false, though probably she never considered those beyond thinking of one or two possibilities, as most of us do in trying to plan. Perhaps we could say she has some concept associated with that sentence, in the sense of a concept not being a fixed thing, not a mental thing nor an object. And that concept gives the way that Suzy hopes; it gives a disposition.

---

[5] If we use "is true" as a predicate of sentences/propositions in our work, we will have to either resolve or avoid the liar paradox. See my "A Theory of Truth Based on a Medieval Solution to the Liar Paradox".

[6] It's not only that we can avoid the problems with viewing "Zoe will call" in (15) as a proposition by saying that it is sentences, not propositions, that are being used as restrictors. My approach is based on a notion of proposition used in all my work: the full development of classical predicate logic, including modifiers and taking account of time and space, as well as in critical thinking and essays on logic as the art of reasoning well. Perhaps all that could be done taking propositions as abstract, ignoring their linguistic representations (if they have any), but I haven't seen even a small part done on those lines.

The dispositions for meaningfulness for using particular words, such as "dog" or "justice", are constrained by norms of our language community. This is what allows us to extend the idea of disposition for meaningfulness to sentences, where perhaps no one previously used "Zoe is a bipedal mammal" nor will use it again. What we have are norms of use—which include but are not limited to grammar—that constrain how we use a sentence and how we understand the sentence.

I think that most of us understand "Zoe will call" not as a scheme of propositions but in terms of how we understand its parts as put together according to our grammar and our norms of use.[7]

Chinese

This view of intentions and meaning seems compatible with what I have learned from Chad Hansen about how pre-Han Chinese spoke and acted.[8] In "Chinese Language, Chinese Philosophy, and 'Truth'" he says:

> I shall argue that classical Chinese philosophy had a different conception of both knowledge and belief. The classical Chinese grammatical structures that we translate as belief expressions were simple two-place predicates—action expressions. I call the expressions "term-belief" contexts. Where Western philosophy of mind dealt with input, procession, and storage of content (data, information), Chinese philosophers portrayed heart-mind as consisting of dispositional attitudes to make distinctions in guiding action. Sentential belief statements represent a relation between a person and a sentence believed. Term-belief, in Chinese, represents a way of responding rather than a propositional attitude.
>
> No single character or conventional string of ancient Chinese corresponds in a straightforward way to "believes that" or "belief that." No string or structure is equivalent to "believe" or "belief" in the formal sense that it takes sentences or propositions as its object. Where English would use a structure such as "King Wen believes that Ch'ang An is beautiful," pre-Han Chinese employed two different structures. The simplest uses the descriptive predicate term as the main verb, "King Wen beautifuls Ch'ang An."
>
> This belief structure of ancient Chinese language signals a different philosophy of mind as well as a different epistemology.

---

[7] Another way to explain meaningfulness might be to return to the medieval analysis of a predicate or proposition having signification but not supposition.

[8] Though not necessarily with how modern Chinese speakers speak and act, he tells me.

It does not generate a picture of some "mental states" with a
sentential, propositional, or representational content. Corresponding
to King Wen's "belief" is a disposition to discriminate among cities.
He discriminates among cities in such a way that Ch'ang An falls on
the beautiful side. "Beautiful-ing" a city involves both linguistic and
non-linguistic dispositions, for example, King Wen's disposition to
classify and distinguish things, to issue orders to his bearers, court
artists, and so forth. The most straightforward evidence that he
discriminates is his tendency to utter "beautiful" when the dialogue
context makes Ch'ang An a topic of discussion. If we think of speech
acts rather than beliefs, we will grasp the action-oriented implications
of term-belief structure. Students of Chinese learn to talk about the
structure as having either a "causative" or "putative" reading. We are
taught to translate the sentence discussed above as either "King Wen
beautified Ch'ang An" or as "King Wen regards Ch'ang An as
beautiful," depending on the context.
    . . . Deeming . . . to be beautiful or "beautiful-ing" are things we
do. They are not merely the "having" of some mental "content." The
dispositional analysis more naturally reflects the syntax of either
term-belief structure than does the mental content analysis. pp. 500–501

And in *A Daoist Theory of Chinese Thought*, Hansen says:

I concentrate on a practical, social conception of language. I avoid
projecting the theory of an inner mental life, consciousness, experience, and any mentalist theory of meaning. I credit all Chinese
philosophers with the view that language is a social mechanism
for shaping human behavior. p. 269

Examples

Example 1 Suzy is afraid that Spot will bite Puff.

Analysis What is the fear that Suzy has? We describe it with a
sentence. Is that the same fear she has that Dick's dog will bite Puff?
Is that the same fear she has that Puff will be bitten? Is that the same
fear she has that Puff will be run over by a car? We can describe these
"fears" only by invoking specific sentences. Then we ask whether the
resulting ways of fearing used as restrictors yield equivalent propositions. In our analysis, we write the example as:

(((— is afraid) / ((((— will bite) / obj (Puff)) (Spot))) (Suzy)

Hopes, fears, desires, expectations, beliefs—we invoke these to
find a thing that is the cause of how Suzy or Dick or Spot is acting. But

to say that "Spot wants to play" is true because Spot has a desire to play is no more than rewriting "Spot wants to play".

Example 2   Dick and Zoe both saw something they thought was a coyote.
Analysis   Some would conclude from the example:

Dick and Zoe had the same thought.

But what is the thought that both Zoe and Dick had? Is it some state of their brains? How do we draw equivalences of brain states? Is it conscious? Is it part of the world outside their mental lives?

These questions seem intractable. But all we need is that how they are thinking is the same, as described by the same sentence used as restrictor.

Example 3   Flo knows that Spot is a dog.
Analysis   We can write this as:

(((— knows) / ((— is a dog) (Spot))) (Flo)

Knowing is something we do. There are ways to know. Knowing is not construed here as requiring a proposition or sentence as object, as in:

Flo knows that "Spot is a dog" is true.

Example 4   Flo knows how to whistle.
Analysis   Here an infinitive is used as a restrictor:

((— knows) / (to whistle)) (Flo, now)

In the Western tradition we distinguish between knowing how and knowing that. But here both are seen as ways of knowing, distinguished only by whether the restrictor of "to know" is an infinitive or a sentence.[9]

Example 5   Dick said that Zeke is a criminal.
Analysis   We can parse this as:

((— said) / ((— is a criminal) (Zeke))) (Dick)

There is no use-mention confusion here. "Zeke is a criminal" is a sentence but not used as a proposition nor as a quoted part of speech. It is used as a restrictor, telling how Dick said.

---

[9] If I understand correctly from Chad Hansen in *A Daoist Theory of Chinese Thought*, pre-Han Chinese philosophers made no distinction between knowing how and knowing that. Indeed, the latter was not even considered, for they used no notion of proposition.

Example 6 *Spot barked that he was hungry.*

Analysis We can parse this as:

((— barked) / ((— is hungry) (Spot))) (Spot)

We don't have to invoke Spot's thoughts or mental states to evaluate this. It's what we do normally: we say he was barking in such a way that we interpret it as showing that he was hungry.

Example 7
- (a) *Walter believes that Marilyn Monroe was an actress.*
- (b) *Marilyn Monroe is Norma Jean Mortensen.*

Therefore
- (c) *Walter believes that Norma Jean Mortensen was an actress.*

Analysis Is the inference valid? Walter doesn't know that Norma Jean Mortensen was Marilyn Monroe, so how could he think that Norma Jean Mortensen was an actress?

Some would say that the terms "Marilyn Monroe" and "Norma Jean Mortensen" are used here intensionally. But all that means is that the truth-values of (a) and (c) depend on some semantic value of "Marilyn Monroe" and "Norma Jean Mortensen" other than their reference(s). In this case, it seems, the evaluations depend on what those terms mean to Walter. But we have no way to grasp that semantic value except to track how the atomic sentences that involve referring to Walter and which have the terms "Marilyn Monroe" and "Norma Jean Mortensen " are evaluated. Or at least I see none. Talk of intensions as opposed to extensions does not clarify here.[10]

We can parse the example:

(a′) ((— believes) / ((— was an actress) (Marilyn Monroe))) (Walter)

(b′) Marilyn Monroe ≡ Norma Jean Mortensen

Therefore,

(c′) ((— believes) / ((— was an actress) (Norma Jean Mortensen))) (Walter)

The inference is not valid because in (a′) and (c′) different restrictors are used. The reference(s) of the names in them is not part of the evaluation of them, for there is no semantic value of these restrictors built

---

[10] See Chapter 13 of *The Internal Structure of Predicates and Names* for a fuller discussion of intensions and extensions.

up from their parts. Believing is something we do, and there are ways we do it.

Example 8 *Dean Furtz respects Dr. E as a teacher but not as a scholar.*

Analysis The example has two propositions joined with "but", which if we are concerned only with truth-values we can treat as "and" joining two propositions:

Dean Furtz respects Dr. E as a teacher.

Dean Furtz does not respect Dr. E as a scholar.

We can write these as:

(a) (((— respects) / ((— is a teacher) (Dr. E))) (Dean Furtz)

(b) (((— respects) / ((— is a scholar) (Dr. E))) (Dean Furtz)

Since the restrictors are different, the truth-values of (a) and (b) need not be the same.[11]

Example 9 *Dick wishes he were rich.*

Analysis We can parse this as:

((— wishes) / ((— is rich) (Dick))) (Dick)

But can "Dick wishes" be true absent any wish?[12]

Example 10 Zoe: How do you feel?
            Dick: *I've got a pain in my shoulder.*
            Zoe: *Me, too.*

---

[11] Compare what Chad Hansen says in "Chinese Language, Chinese Philosophy, and "Truth"":

> The Mohists were testing the theory of inference which said that a *shih* base will always produce a *jan* result. They rejected the theory using argument by counterexample. Most of the counter-examples use intentional phrases; for example, the Mohist says that while her younger brother is a handsome man, her loving her younger brother is not her loving a handsome man (she loves her brother qua brother, not qua handsome man). They designed the entire essay to license departure from the inference scheme. The departure was important to a famous paradox of Mohist social-political theory; thieves are men but killing thieves is not killing men. p. 510

[12] See my "The Twenty-First or "Lost" Sophism on Self-Reference of John Buridan" in this volume.

Analysis Is the pain that Dick has the same as the pain Zoe has? Can I feel the pain you have in your foot? Can anyone feel my pain? We are led to ask these questions when we treat pains as things.

But Zoe is asking how Dick feels. He could say that he feels bad, or he feels happy, or he feels hungry. Or he feels pain-in-my-shoulder. That's to treat pain-in-my-shoulder as a way of feeling. We can parse the example as:

(— feels) / (pain / in (shoulder) / of (Dick)) (Dick)

Whether you can feel my pain becomes a question of whether you can feel the same way I do. For that we look to behavior rather than inaccessible mental states. Compare:

(— feels) / (pain / in (shoulder) / of (Dick)) (Zoe)

Conclusion

We can understand talk of intentions without invoking mental objects, or different notions of propositions, or intensional contexts. There are ways of hoping, wanting, trying, and knowing, rather than objects of hoping, wanting, trying, and knowing.

Some invoke how we speak as a major criterion in evaluating the acceptability of an analysis. This is part of a view that English "gets it right". How could we be wrong about the nature of the world? How can our grammar mislead us? It's not that we have been wrong but that there can be other ways to parse the world.[13] I am not suggesting that we replace our ordinary talk. Rather, I am trying to get clearer about our web of inferences and meaning.

But we often do talk this way when we talk about what dogs want or know. We infer from behavior for them, as we do with us. We look at how they act, not what they think. But behavior is not enough. It's true now that I wish I were a millionaire, but if I had not told you, there is nothing in my behavior that would clue you to it.

Nor is this analysis meant to replace current Western metaphysics of hopes and desires, thoughts and intentions. It is an alternative metaphysics, minimal in that it invokes human capabilities but not mental objects.

---

[13] See my *Language and the World*.

REFERENCES

EPSTEIN, Richard L.
- 1992 A Theory of Truth Based on a Medieval Solution to the Liar Paradox
  History and Philosophy of Logic, 13, 1992, pp. 149-177.
- 2016 *The Internal Structure of Predicates and Names*
  Advanced Reasoning Forum
- 2022 *Time and Space in Formal Logic*
  Advanced Reasoning Forum
- 2021 *Language and the World: Essays New and Old*
  Advanced Reasoning Forum

HANSEN, Chad
- 1985 Chinese Language, Chinese Philosophy, and "Truth"
  Journal of Asian Studies, vol. XLIV, no. 3, pp. 491–519.
- 1992 *A Daoist Theory of Chinese Thought*
  Oxford University Press.

Numbers?

We begin by picking out.

        an apple   an apple

Instead of "an" we can and do use the word "one" or the numeral "1".

        1 apple   **1** apple

But "1" by itself has no significance beyond "an": it's just pointing to a thing. It begins to have significance when we count to answer "How many apples?"

        1 apple   **2** apple

We use written numerals or sounds associated with those to count. Writing in English, I start from the left. There are 2 (two) apples.

    Now let's look at:

224   *Numbers?*

an apple   an apple   an apple

We now have:

1 apple   **2** apple   **1** apple

To answer "How many apples?" we count, again starting from the left, using a new word/symbol to continue our counting.

1 apple   **2** apple   **3** apple

See, there are three (3) apples.
    We've just discovered:

    2 apples and 1 apple make 3 apples

Let's simplify how we'll say and write this by using "+" to indicate we're meant to continue the counting and by using "=" for the result of the counting.

2 apples + 1 apple = 3 apples

If I were an Arabic writer, I'd start from the right:

3 apple   **2** apple   **1** apple

We've just discovered:

1 apple + 2 apples = 3 apples

So we have:

2 apples + 1 apple = 1 apple + 2 apples = 3 apples

Let's check to see how this works when we count lemons.

1 lemon   **2** lemon   **3** lemon

3 lemon   **2** lemon   **1** lemon

226   Numbers?

So we have:

> 2 lemons + 1 lemon = 1 lemon + 2 lemons = 3 lemons

Based on just these two examples, we confidently make the leap to conclude that it doesn't matter in what order we count:

> 2 of any kind + 1 of that kind = 3 of that kind
>
> 1 of any kind + 2 of that kind = 3 of that kind

So 2 of any kind + 1 of that kind = 1 of any kind + 2 of that kind

Going to my refrigerator, I found ingredients for another example.

    an apple   an apple   an orange

How many? We count as before:

    1 apple   **2** apple   **1** orange

Now how many? "How many what?" 2 apples and 1 orange make . . . ? Oh, easy, we switch to "pieces of fruit". There are 3 pieces of fruit.

1 piece of fruit   **2** piece of fruit   **3** piece of fruit

This is fun! I wish you were here in my living room to continue this experiment with me.

1 apple   **2** apple   **1** lemon **1** lemon   **1** orange

We can answer "How many?" by counting pieces of fruit.

1 piece of fruit   **2** piece of fruit   **3** piece of fruit
                                              4 piece of fruit   **5** piece of fruit

This is getting hard to put on a page. And it's tedious repeating "piece of fruit". Let's drop the label, since we know we're counting pieces of fruit.

1   **2**   **3**   **4**   **5**

The answer to "How many?" is "5", knowing we mean "5 pieces of fruit". Now how many?

We've got an apple, another apple, an avocado, a grapefruit, a lemon, a lemon, and an orange. It looks like we have:

    1   **2**   **3**   **4** **5**   **6**   **7**

Seven (7) pieces of fruit. Yes, a grapefruit is a fruit. But wait. Is an avocado a fruit? Aren't fruits sweet? No, or rather yes, it is a fruit, I've seen avocados growing on a tree. There are seven pieces of fruit. But is that big one in the back a grapefruit? I'm not sure now. So I'll cut it.

Oops. It's a big orange, not a grapefruit. I must have picked the wrong one when I went shopping. A big orange looks a lot like a grapefruit. But that doesn't change our counting: there are seven (7) pieces of fruit. But wait. There are no longer seven (7) pieces of fruit: there are eight (8) (count 'em). Or perhaps we should say that there are six (6) whole pieces of fruit and two (2) pieces of a fruit.

Rummaging in my cupboard, I continue to experiment.

We pick out an apple, another apple, and a tin can. "How many?" How many what? 1 apple, 2 apples, 3 . . . what? Not apples, not pieces of fruit. We grasp for a kind of thing that will include apples and a tin can. My buddy (and perhaps you if you were here) jumps right in and says "physical things". There are 3 (three) physical things.

But is "physical things" a kind we can use for counting? What are the physical things in that picture? I got adventurous and . . .

I took the lid off the can. So there are four (4) physical things there now. Right? But wait, the lid was there before, just not detached. So before there were three undetached physical things, and now there are four. But here's another photo I took a moment later from above.

230   Numbers?

Can you see? There are beans in the can, lots of beans. How many? I can't count them without disturbing the can. So I can't answer "How many?"

Oh, this is just silly. Let's stick with just pieces of fruit.

Now how many? All fruit there. 1 apple, 2 apples, 3 . . . what? That's a bunch of grapes. Does it count as a (one) fruit? Or should we count each grape? That bunch of grapes has been in the refrigerator a long time, way too long, and some of the grapes are squishy and no longer round(ish). Should I count each of those? That's too much trouble. There are three (3) pieces or bunches of fruit. To count, all we have to do is get clear about what kind of things we're counting. It doesn't even make sense to ask how many physical things there are in the picture. Do we count the stem of each apple? The woody stem of the grapes? Each branching of that woody stem?

We can't answer "How many?" without first saying what we are paying attention to. Or perhaps implicitly knowing what we're paying attention to, as in the first picture: apples, not stems of apples. Our lives, our experience, our language direct us to what we can and do pay attention to—until we get to the apples and the tin can and we have to grasp for a more general kind. We know now that we can't use "physical thing" as a kind. So in that picture to answer "How many?" we say "2 apples and 1 tin can". So there are three (3) apples-or-tin cans, and in the last picture there are three (3) pieces of fruit-or-bunches of fruit.

If we can agree on what we're counting, we can establish some rules for counting. From our few examples, we have:

2 of anything and 1 more of that kind of thing is 3 of that kind of thing.

1 of anything and 2 more of that kind of thing is 3 of that kind of thing.

As before, let's write "+" for joining the counting and "=" for marking the result of the counting:

(*) 2 of anything + 1 of that kind of thing = 3 of that kind of thing

   1 of anything + 2 of that kind of thing = 3 of that kind of thing

But we've left out "more of": 1 more of that kind of thing. That's pretty obvious, so let's just agree to remember that.

We're convinced this holds for counting any kind of thing. How about drops of water? With an eye dropper I'll drop onto a plate on my table one (1) drop of water, then another drop of water, then another drop of water.

2 drops of water + 1 drop of water = 3 drops of water ????

> With an eyedropper I dropped one drop of water onto a plate — same background of the towel. Then I dropped another drop of water onto the plate, same place, and got a bigger drop of water on the plate. Then I dropped another drop of water onto the plate and got a still bigger drop of water on the plate. But water is transparent, so I couldn't get a good photo. Drops of tea are too transparent to photograph, too. So you'll have to trust me that in the end there was just one big drop of water on the plate. Or better yet, do the experiment for yourself. It's fun!

232   Numbers?

No, we have just one big drop of water. Whatever we meant by "+" in (*), it can't mean this. What exactly does it mean? The things we are counting must have some stability, some persistence in time as distinct things in the process of counting for us to count them. That's why the kind of counting in (*) doesn't work for drops of water, for clouds, for mud, for electrons. Still, if we remember that these numerals are meant for counting kinds of things that have persistence in time, we have (*).

Now look. Wow! Lots of lemons. Let's count:

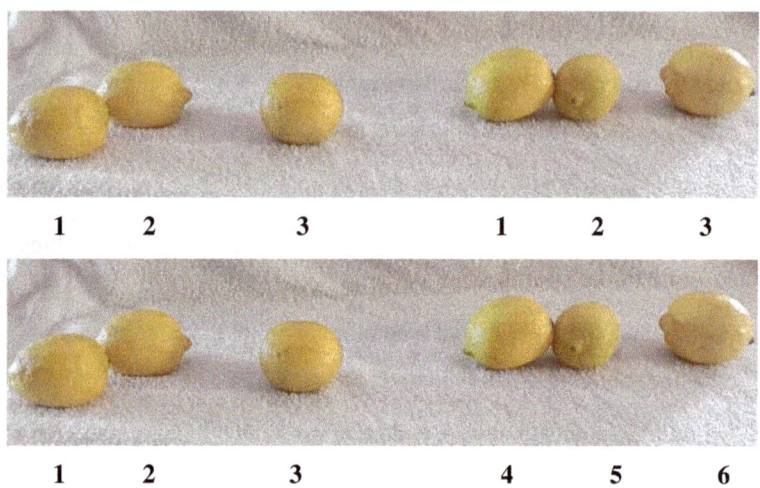

So we have:

   2 times (2 + 1) = 6 lemons

By "times" I just mean we repeat the counting. We can summarize, using "×" for "times":

(‡)
   2 + 1 = 1 + 2 = 3

   2 × (2 + 1) = 6

Or at least we can if we keep in mind that these are numerals for counting things of a specific kind of thing, any specific kind of thing. In this manner (and I'll leave a long exposition to you), we can develop arithmetic for counting things of a kind.

Now (‡) is so clear, so easy to remember, that we take it to have some independence of kinds of things. And it does, so long as we don't forget that the counting is for a kind of thing that has some stability:

3 birds
14 trees
6 avocados

And we blithely use our counting for other "kinds of things":

5 ideas
82 instances of evil
14 sunsets

We do this (in part) because we have nouns for these: "ideas", "instances of evil", "sunsets". That's because English is a thing-language (see my *Language and the World*) which leads us to parse the world as made up (primarily) of things, so we even think of clouds as things. We classify nouns into ones for things we can count (count nouns) that take a plural, like "idea", and ones for . . . well, not things but masses (mass nouns), like "mud" and "water". To count mud we have to use what linguists call "a classifier" to tell us what "things" of that kind we're counting, for example, patches of mud. To count water, we have to use "a classifier" to tell us what "things" of that kind we're counting, for example, puddles of water. Yet we have the classifier "drop of" for water that we saw doesn't work for counting. Our language directs us, but it isn't always reliable.

The numerals 1, 2, 3, . . . can be used for counting any kind of things that have some persistence. They are adjectives. We manipulate them without the labels for the kind of thing as at (‡) above, not even the general "of the same kind of thing", because it's easy. But then we start to view them as having some independence of the kinds of things, and ask "What do the numerals stand for?" And we answer "Numbers".

What are numbers? In 2,500 years no one has come up with an answer that satisfies most people. The reason we cannot agree on what numbers are is because we've begun to read adjectives as nouns. What does "large" stand for? What does "tall" stand for? We might answer "a concept". But what is the concept of **1**? Is it a state of my mind? Of your mind? Some free-floating "entity" that is shared by all our minds? Do there even have to be minds for there to be concepts? Do we have to elaborate an analysis of concepts to justify "2 + 1 = 3" without labels?

One apparently simple answer is offered by the platonist. A platonist is someone who believes that there are things that are not perceptible to us by our senses, not of time and space, but which can be apprehended only by our intellects. So "7", the numeral, stands for the number 7, which is not of the physical world but through our intellects we can apply to things of our experience. But consider:

$$1 + 1 = 2$$

There is "1" standing for the number, which I have to write as "1", since though we'll go along with the platonist here, we still have to communicate. So to get the addition of 1 + 1, there has to be not one but two "1"s. Each is perceptible to us only through our intellects, not our senses: *not* through sight, smell, taste, hearing, touch, location in space, location in time. But how can I tell which of the "1"s I am apprehending? How can I count if they are completely indistinguishable? And what cannot be distinguished is one, not two.

The problem with the platonist's conception of numbers is not that there cannot be abstract objects—after all, I can't prove there aren't abstract objects any more than the platonist can prove there are. The problem is that if there are abstract objects, then trying to use those as the basis of arithmetic is incoherent. We can't lead from the real, physical, perceptible of arithmetic to the abstract; and we can't apply the abstract to the real, physical, perceptible.

Some mathematicians say that numbers can be defined in set theory. But as soon as we try to say what they mean we get stuck. The empty set, Ø, is zero? Or it stands for zero? The empty set is nothing, so we have zero is nothing, and nothing is not something, in particular nothing is not a number. Then the set with just the empty set in it, {Ø}, is what "1" stands for. Or we should say that {Ø} is 1? And then the set with just 1 in it is what "2" stands for: {{Ø}}. Or should we say that 2 is {{Ø}}? But others say that the procession of numbers is: {Ø}, {Ø, {Ø}}, {Ø, {Ø},{Ø, {Ø}}},.... . Which is right? Which are really numbers? A silly question, for there is nothing other than convenience for use in formal set theories to recommend one over the other. Yet the formal set theories in which they are presented are not equivalent. Unless you believe that sets are real, these "numbers" are not things at all but only notations to give a "foundation" for arithmetic. (See Paul Benacerraf's "What Numbers Could Not Be", in Benacerraf and Putnam, *Philosophy of Mathematics: Selected Readings*; that has articles on other answers to "What are numbers?")

What is accomplished by viewing numerals as nouns rather than adjectives? They give us some mental crutch to allow us to make manipulations like:

17 + 22 = 39

17 + 22 = 22 + 17

3 x (8 + 7) = (3 x 8) + (3 x 7) = (8+ 7) x 3 = 45

But what a high price we pay for that mental crutch. We enter into a never-never land of "numbers". We forget the genesis of arithmetic and create conundrums for ourselves ("How many 17s are there?", "Which set really is 23 ?"). It's not just that we don't need numbers for arithmetic. It's that we can't figure out what such "things" are beyond giving us a mental crutch.

But the platonist and others who hold that numbers are real say that numerals cannot be the basis for arithmetic because there are only finitely many of them. So we ask, what do you mean by "finite"?

We can extend the list of numerals as far as we want. We have the base numerals:

1 2 3 4 5 6 7 8 9

Then rather than using a further base numeral to extend the counting, we use the idea of a place holder. When we write two numerals together, like "39", we say that the first numeral tells us how many tens, and the second how many ones. For this we need a new numeral, "0", which we call "zero". It is used to indicate: none (of the kind we're counting). So in the very first photo above, we can answer "How many lemons?" by saying "0". There are no lemons. Then "10", which we read as "ten", indicates the next in the counting after the sequence above. And we can continue:

1 2 3 4 5 6 7 8 9 10 11 12 13 14 15 16 17 18 19 20

To continue past "99" we say that the first place in the numeral "382" stands for how many ten times ten there are, and call ten times ten "a hundred". And if there are four places in the numeral, the first numeral stands for how many ten times ten times ten there are, which we call "a thousand". This is a particularly easy way to continue counting— certainly easier than the Roman method of using a different base numeral for each higher order of tens, or the Babylonians using twelve base numerals and no zero. The invention of the use of "0" was a major aid in using counting, though we get tongue tied if we try to say what it stands for. It stands for nothing— but that sounds as if we are treating nothing as a thing. But it isn't a thing; zero just marks that no counting can even begin. No lemon, no apple, no tin can. Nothing mysterious there (see the entry "Nothing" by P. L. Heath in *The Encyclopedia of Philosophy* edited by Paul Edwards).

We can even program a machine to start "counting", that is, generating numerals in order, and get really "big" numerals. Or we can designate someone to continue the list after the current writer dies, and then another after that, and . . . . Operationally there is no difference between there being an upper limit for numerals that can never be reached and an infinite "list" of numerals—that ". . .". Mathematicians say we need a completed infinity of numbers to do mathematics, to put on a sound foundation the theory of real analysis, on which is based all the mathematics that we use to build cars, plot the trajectories of rocket ships, to do almost all the calculations we need. That's wrong. We use completed infinities because it makes the analysis easier. But it's no "solid foundation" for mathematics to start with a belief in completed infinite collections which live in the same world as fairies and demons and unicorns and Santa Claus. It's just that completed infinite collections are useful as abstractions that make our calculations easier (see my "Mathematics as the Art of Abstraction"). And in any case, it's not clear that we need to imagine infinitely many numbers rather than abstract to infinitely many numerals. And taking numerals rather than numbers as basic clarifies and de-mystifies a lot. It brings arithmetic back to our lives and world; arithmetic is a human activity. We develop arithmetic with experiments.

Experiments? Yes, though it all seems so obvious we think not. We think that $1 + 2 = 3$ is a truth of all time, all places, incontrovertible, true just by the meaning of the symbols ("analytic" the philosophers say). But it's not, as we saw with the experiment with drops of water. "Baloney" I get in response from some philosophers and mathematicians. "That's not what's meant by '$1 + 2 = 3$'." So what is meant? I put it in terms of counting. And the experiment showed that the things we are counting have to have some stability, some persistence in time. As with all scientific theories, we find the range of application of the theory by devising experiments that could make it false. "$1 + 2 = 3$" is true not because of the meaning of the terms. It is not universal. We take it as universally true because we reject any counterexample, any experiment that shows it's false by saying "That's not what I meant; that is not it, at all."

We learn arithmetic as children with just such experiments (it would be great if we could get kids to eat the apples and oranges and grapes at the end of those instead of the candy that rich corporations purvey to them). And the experiments, the "truths" of arithmetic begin to seem so solid, so basic, so permanent and right that we forget that we had to learn them. They are built into our language, whether English, Spanish, Dutch, Romanian, Portuguese, German—what Benjamin Lee Whorf called "Standard Average European" (SAE) languages. Basic to those, and perhaps to all Indo-European languages, is the view that the world is made up of things, things that persist in time. That is reflected in the grammatical category of count nouns, ones that have a plural form. Our language leads us to relegate to a secondary status any conception of the world as mass, as flow, as process, for which we have the grammatical categories of mass nouns and, in English, gerunds ("running", "barking"). Some languages have built into their grammar a view of the world as mass-process, the flow of all, as you can read in *Language and the World*. Some of those allow what they describe as water or mud to be further described as divided into parts using classifiers, as we do with "a lake of water", "a patch of mud". Some, though, have almost no focus on individual things, and no arithmetic, for there are no individual things to count in their speakers' conceptions. There is no right or wrong about it. Simply, arithmetic as we know it is not universal, not to be "discovered", but is a process we derive from our grammar. Unless, that is, you say that SAE languages "get it right", really describe the world correctly (more or less), and those "odd" languages, originally spoken by many other peoples, get it wrong. How can't they see that the world is made up of things?

We invent and use numerals to count, to answer "How many?" Numbers are a fiction, perhaps a useful one, that arise by leaving off the labels for saying what kind of things we are counting. No mystery.

Numerals are adjectives, not nouns.

Appendix: *Experiments in arithmetic*

A basic condition for an experiment to be good—that is, reliable for drawing inferences about the subject—is that it be duplicable (see my "Reasoning in the Sciences"). So let's test that the experiments I described above can be duplicated.

I didn't have much of the fruit I started with (hunger and self-indulgence). So I went to the grocery store and got some more.

1 piece of fruit   **2** piece of fruit   **3** piece of fruit

So, **2** pieces of fruit + **1** piece of fruit = **3** pieces of fruit

1 piece of fruit   **2** piece of fruit   **1** bunch of fruit

(‡) **2** pieces of fruit + **1** bunch of fruit = **3** pieces of fruit or bunch of fruit

It seems it doesn't matter if we change the fruits. Except here it's not obvious that we shouldn't also count the stem of the grapes. And when I moved the bunch of grapes I got:

Some of the grapes came off the stems and I collected them. Now (‡) seems wrong, even though there's still the same "stuff" that was there before. What is it we're counting? And why doesn't the color of the apples matter?

Pressing on, let's duplicate another of our experiments in counting.

Just like before. No, that's a different brand of kidney beans. Does that matter? How do we know if we don't count the beans in the can? Better to be safe and get the same brand.

Yep, that's the same brand. But it's pinto beans, not kidney beans. Does that qualify as a duplication? Here's another try:

Whoa! That's a really big can of beans.

What's important? What's important is what we are paying attention to. These attempts to duplicate the earlier experiment have the same ingredients: apples and tin cans. We would count it a duplication even if we put in a big can of tomatoes. Even a can of motor oil would do. That's because we've chosen what matters by saying the kind of objects we are counting: apples and tin cans. Or we could say fruit and tin cans, and then do the experiment with two oranges and a can of motor oil. It doesn't matter that the towel is draped a bit differently in the last photos and has been washed and dried (I used it after a shower).

We build into our experiments what we deem to be a result (compare dice rolling: in a casino if one of the dice lands on its edge, it doesn't count as a "roll of the dice"). And in the case of arithmetic, we build into our experiments the grammar of our language, not least because we count things of a particular kind, that is, things that can be described by a count noun or some disjunction of count nouns (pieces of fruit-or-cans; patches of mud). But then what about . . .

As before, two (2) apples and an (1) orange. Only I got hungry and ate part of one of the apples. Does it still count as an apple? It's not just what we have standard words for in our language; we can pay attention by picking out using some compound pieces of language, here "half-eaten apple".

We cannot falsify a "scientific truth" if we won't allow an experiment that has a different metaphysical basis. Philosophers in the Western tradition since Aristotle take as granted that there are things in the world that have stability through "their changes" and then try to understand how we can come to know those things. After all, see the apple is red, no wait, the sun is setting, and now "the apple" looks gray. Is it "really" red? And the next day, having been left out, it's brown and mushy. There's no problem for someone who views the world through a mass-process language. There is no apple-thing, but only apple-ing, changing but not changing because change is what we ascribe to things, only flowing in the flow of all. And hence, for a speaker of such a language, no obvious route to arithmetic.

The Twenty-First or "Lost" Sophism on Self-Reference of John Buridan

The discovery of the twenty-first or "lost" sophism of John Buridan on self-reference and the nature of wishes is recounted, and the sophism is translated.

Introduction

I worked with the late George Hughes when he was translating the *Sophismata* of John Buridan on self-reference.[1] Stimulated by his work and discussions with him I later devised a modern theory of truth based on Buridan's ideas.[2]

I had heard that there was one more sophism on self-reference that concluded Chapter 8 of Buridan's *Sophismata*. References to it in medieval literature were scant and unclear, suggesting only that there was a twenty-first, or what came to be called " the lost sophism," which was said to be about self-reference and wishes.

In my peregrinations I worked at the University da Paraíba in João Pessoa, Brazil, and there I was surprised to find several medieval works on parchment. All were in a very bad state of conservation. I was able to make a hand copy of part of one that appeared to refer to John Buridan on self-reference. My competence in medieval Latin is very poor. However, in the last year I was able to work with someone to translate the text and now believe that it is indeed the lost sophism of John Buridan.

I present my translation here. The terminology and presentation are meant to follow that established by George Hughes.

The 21st or Lost Sophism of John Buridan on Self-Reference

Sophism 21
Star light, star bright,
First star I see tonight,
I wish I may, I wish I might,
Have this wish I wish tonight.

The posited case is that Plato utters these words upon observing the first star of the evening, and this is all he says or thinks that evening before going to sleep. The question is whether Plato has made a wish.

21.1 Argument that Plato has wished:

Plato has wished. He has wished that he may have the wish he is now making, for he has wished that he might have the wish he has tonight, and he is now wishing. Thus he has wished.

21.1.1 Moreover, his wish is fulfilled. He has no other wishes so his only wish is to have his wish. Surely a wish is fulfilled if it is not unfulfilled, and the posited case and Plato's wish, which exists and we showed is a wish, together entail that it is impossible that Plato's wish be unfulfilled.

21.2 Argument that Plato has not wished:

Plato has not wished for anything. He has only wished that he have a wish fulfilled, but that wish is a wish for a wish. Since Plato has not wished for anything, he cannot have his wish fulfilled.

21.3 My own view is that Plato has not wished, and therefore that he cannot have his wish come true. That is because he has not wished for anything.

21.3.1 I understand "for anything" to mean that there is some condition which can fulfill the wish. That is, for an expression to be a wish there must be a proposition which, if true, would constitute fulfillment of the wish.

21.3.1.1 But then is a wish that a circle be a square a wish? By the definition above it is, since it is a wish that "A circle is a square" be true. That this is an impossibility means only that the wish is unfulfillable, not that it is not a wish. The conditions for its fulfillment are clear; it simply cannot be satisfied. A wish for an impossibility, which we call an impossible wish, is still a wish.

21.3.2 But Plato's utterance is not an impossible wish. Because it is self-referential it does not express a wish at all.

21.3.2.1 It seems to be a wish, but it can only be a wish that it be itself fulfilled, as Plato has made no other wish that evening. The conditions for its fulfillment appear to be expressed by the proposition "The wish is fulfilled" which leads us, *ad infinitum*, again and again to the wish itself.

21.3.2.2 You argue as above that this does not mean the wish has no conditions of fulfillment, only that its conditions for fulfillment are trivial. Anything will fulfill the condition, since nothing would constitute falsifying the proposition.

21.3.2.3 But I say that "a subject and predicate stand for the same" is an affirmative condition which in this case could not be shown to hold. The predicate has no supposition, even though it has signification.

21.4 You may, however, choose to make a distinction, saying a wish that is not an impossible wish but is merely unfulfillable due to self-reference is a wishy-washy wish. In that case I concede that Plato has made a wishy-washy wish but that he cannot have his wish fulfilled.

21.5 But then is Plato's wish necessarily a wishy-washy wish? No, for he might have said immediately after uttering it the sentence, "I wish I were Socrates." Then Plato would have made a wish, namely that the wish "I wish I were Socrates" be fulfilled. That is, that the proposition "Plato is Socrates" be true.

21.6 How then can Plato make a wish that expresses the same thought as the sophism yet is really a wish?

21.6.1 In the case of a possibly wishy-washy wish one can express the same wish while ensuring that it is not wishy-washy by simply wishing that the purported wish be indeed a wish.

21.6.2 Thus, what Plato should say to make a wish and not a wishy-washy wish is:

> Star light, star bright,
> First star I see tonight,
> I wish I may, I wish I might,
> Have this wish I wish tonight.
> And if this wish I make tonight
> Is wishy-washy, make it right.

Notes

1. George Hughes, *John Buridan on Self-Reference,* Cambridge University Press, 1982.

2. "A Theory of Truth Based on a Medieval Solution to the Liar Paradox", *History and Philosophy of Logic*, 13, pp. 149-177, 1992, later revised as Chapter XXII of my *Classical Mathematical Logic*, Princeton University Press, 2006.

213637093 (History and Philosophy of Logic) A decision has been made on your submission

1 message

History and Philosophy of Logic <em@editorialmanager.com>
Reply-To: History and Philosophy of Logic <volker.peckhaus@upb.de>
To: Richard L Epstein <rle@advancedreasoningforum.org>

Sat, Dec 25, 2021 at 5:14 AI

Dec 25, 2021

Ref.: Ms. No. THPL-2021-0074
213637093
The Twenty-First or "'Lost'" Sophism on Self-Reference of John Buridan
History and Philosophy of Logic

Dear Richard L. Epstein,

the paper cannot be accepted for the review procedure due to formal reasons: The source for Buridan's sophism is not given (manuscript, library). The Latin version is not given. The person helping to translate is not given. The style is too personal.

Thank you for considering History and Philosophy of Logic. I hope the outcome of this specific submission will not discourage you from the submission of future manuscripts.

Yours sincerely

Volker Peckhaus
Editor in Chief
History and Philosophy of Logic

The Procrastination Paradox

One of us is a serious procrastinator. He can make the day go by looking over his shoulder for the tasks he needs to do to come creeping up on him. It makes him unhappy, but he can't stop.

We want to help him. How can we get him not to procrastinate? Discussing it with him, he came up with a great plan:

> He will write on his calendar for tomorrow:
> "From 8 a.m. to noon procrastinate."

Or at least it seemed like a great plan when he first said it. But then we got to thinking . . .

(1) If tomorrow morning he doesn't procrastinate, then he won't have done what he set himself to do. He's put it off. That is, he will have procrastinated procrastinating. So he will have procrastinated.

(2) But if he does do what he put on his calendar, then he will have procrastinated.

So either way he will procrastinate. He has fixed the future just by writing down on his calendar what he plans to do.

Note that (1) is because procrastinating is idempotent:

procrastinating procrastinating = procrastinating.

But with (2), is procrastinating when you're supposed to procrastinate, procrastinating?

Can anyone suggest a way to help him out of this predicament?

Notes

"He should drink a lot of wine the night before and go to bed at 4 a.m. and sleep through the morning. " But perhaps this is procrastinating if he made the choice to drink and sleep late in order not to procrastinate.

Procrastinating is a conscious choice. Or is it?

　　—I'm sorry I didn't take out the trash this morning. I just forgot about it.
　　—Sure you forgot.

You can't procrastinate doing something you can't do. I can't procrastinate walking to town 50 km away tomorrow morning. Though I can procrastinate thinking about whether I should plan to walk to town.

www.ingramcontent.com/pod-product-compliance
Lightning Source LLC
Chambersburg PA
CBHW071153160426
43196CB00011B/2064